YIDDISHE
KOP

YIDDISHE KOP

CREATIVE PROBLEM SOLVING
IN JEWISH LEARNING, LORE,
AND HUMOR

RABBI NILTON BONDER

Translated from the Portuguese by Diane Grosklaus

SHAMBHALA
Boston & London
1999

Shambhala Publications, Inc.
Horticultural Hall
300 Massachusetts Avenue
Boston, Massachusetts 02115
http://www.shambhala.com

9 8 7 6 5 4 3 2 1

First Edition

Printed in the United States of America

⊗ This edition is printed on acid-free paper that meets the
American National Standards Institute Z39.48 Standard.

Distributed in the United States by Random House, Inc.,
and in Canada by Random House of Canada Ltd.

Library of Congress Cataloging-In-Publication Data

Bonder, Nilton.
    [Idiche kop. English]
    Yiddishe kop: creative problem solving in Jewish learning, lore,
and humor / Nilton Bonder; translated from the Portuguese by Diane
Grosklaus.—1st ed.
        p.   cm.
    ISBN 1-57062-448-8 (alk. paper)
    1. Problem solving—Religious aspects—Judaism.   2. Judaism—
Apologetic works.   3. Ignorance (Theory of knowledge)   I. Title.
BM565.B6513   1999
296.6'8—dc21
                                                    98-54851
                                                        CIP

For my daughter, Alice

What makes it so hard to decide
is not knowing what we want
and how much we want it.

CONTENTS

WISDOM
THE APPARENT REALM OF WHAT IS HIDDEN

REVERENCE
THE HIDDEN REALM OF WHAT IS HIDDEN

EPILOGUE

INTRODUCTION

This book is about problem solving. It draws on an ancient tradition whose history has been plagued by endless problems and hardships. Necessity is the mother of invention—and of solutions. In this case, circumstances permitted the evolution of an astute, shrewd way of looking at life—an approach that Jews call *yiddishe kop*, literally, "Jewish head." *Yiddishe kop* is neither a method nor a system of knowledge, but the accumulation of a minimal "critical mass" of problems needed to trigger a conscious, existential process of questioning the notion of impossible. *Yiddishe kop* represents the turning point at which, after having given up hope, you recover the twinkle in your eye and dare to jump back into the game. It is that unique capacity to turn the tables and checkmate your opponent when you're up against the wall, to reject conventional thinking that keeps you stuck in a losing position and reframe yourself as a master of options that you simply hadn't thought of before.

The solutions produced by *yiddishe kop* remind me of the old Flash Gordon serials, where episodes often ended with our hero in extreme danger, seemingly beyond the point of rescue. We were convinced: "Now he's had it—there's no way out." By the time the next episode was aired, we had gone over all the possible means of escape and found none. Of course we felt we had been tricked when the story began with a replay of the final moments of the previous episode, only now a totally new element was introduced—a rope, a weapon, a hidden ally. We were sure that this element that enabled our hero to escape had not appeared in the original scene. It is precisely this kind of blindness that prevents people from recognizing the factors that make for novel solutions—and that perhaps explains the audacity of certain producers and directors.

The hidden option is the one that we don't see when we first find ourselves up against a problem. When we manage to break the bonds of standard solutions, we are surprised to discover these hidden windows.

Take the solution of a classic problem in geometry: a given point on a two-dimensional plane cannot meet another point on this plane without passing through intermediate points on the plane. What seems impossible when viewed in two dimensions becomes possible when reframed in a three-dimensional context, where that same point can now reach the other point on the same plane by traveling through the third dimension.

Or take Steven Spielberg's film *Raiders of the Lost Ark*: at an especially suspenseful moment, with the damsel in dire distress, the hero is challenged by a brawny wrestler deftly wielding a saber. Entranced by that mighty obstacle, the audience is surprised when the hero puts an end to the problem by simply whipping out his gun.

To an outside observer, the simplicity of a solution unlimited by our addiction to habit patterns and conventions—that is, a solution not biased by the deceptive "aesthetics" of what first comes to mind—may seem even comical. A *yiddishe kop* is attained not so much through knowledge as through transcending a certain ignorance. There once was a television quiz show in which a contestant enclosed in a booth would have to choose a prize without knowing exactly what was being offered. "Will you trade a brand-new car for an old boot?" the host would ask, and the person in the booth would confidently answer "Yes," much to the audience's delight. Being inside the booth—representing deafness, blindness, or ignorance—led participants to make absurd choices. Those outside our own "booths," or conditionings, might observe much the same thing if they were to follow us around for a day.

Yiddishe kop could be translated as the moment when the fog of this ignorance dissipates. Its strength derives from the prospect of survival. Just as a dog defends itself by biting and a cat by scratching, Jews have learned to defend themselves by reframing situations to unveil amazing options. As survivors, they reaffirm and celebrate their successes.

"Impossibility" is always a transitory condition—and whoever knows this won't give up. No other attitude fuels as much creativity or intuition as the decision not to give up. The simple fact that you choose to stay in the game affords possibilities that quite obviously will not exist for someone who has thrown in the towel.

This story comes from the Middle Ages:

A child was found dead in a village. A Jew was immediately accused of committing the crime and of using the victim in some macabre ritual. Thrown in prison, the man knew he was a scapegoat and stood no chance at the forthcoming trial. He asked to see a rabbi and was granted his request.

When the rabbi arrived, he found the man in despair over the death sentence that he was sure awaited him. The rabbi comforted him: "Don't ever believe there is no way out. The Evil One himself, God forbid, will tempt you with that thought."

"But what shall I do?" asked the anguished man.

"Just don't give up, and you will be shown a way out."

When the day of the trial arrived, the judge wanted to pretend that the accused would be allowed a fair trial and a chance to prove his innocence, so he said to the prisoner:

"Since you Jews have faith, I will let the Lord decide this matter. On one piece of paper I will write the word 'innocent' and on another one, 'guilty.' You will pick one, and the Lord will decide your destiny."

As the Jew had guessed, the judge prepared two pieces of paper with the word "guilty" on both of them. Normally we would say that the chances of the accused had dropped from fifty to zero percent—there was no way he could select the piece of paper saying "innocent," since there was no such paper.

Recalling the rabbi's words, the prisoner meditated for a moment. Suddenly his eyes lit up with a new spark. He grabbed one of the pieces of paper and swallowed it in a gulp. The witnesses were upset: "Why did you do that? How will we know your destiny now?"

"Easy," answered the Jew. "Just read what it says on the other paper, and you will know that I chose the opposite."

We discover that this man's chances were only zero percent if viewed within certain confines. Through a cunning born of necessity, he created a new context in which his chances of overcoming adversity jumped from zero to one hundred percent. In other words, reframing the situation made it possible to turn reality upside down.

The purpose of this book is to study Judaism's intimate relationship with the process of reframing—the secrets of which, in fact, lie at the very core of Judaism's proclivity for observing reality with caution. Since ancient times, the kabbalistic tradition has maintained that reality is layered, like an onion. By peeling off layers one by one, we can dissect reality much more effectively than if we perceive only one facet of it.

The four parts of this book are based on the idea that reality can be divided into four worlds, or four dimensions. What I offer is not so much a method for discovering solutions as a way of breaking out of structures of ignorance that fail to take into account the various aspects of reality.

These four worlds are represented by the four dimensions described by the Alter Rebbe:[1]

1. The Apparent Realm of What Is Apparent
2. The Hidden Realm of What Is Apparent
3. The Apparent Realm of What Is Hidden
4. The Hidden Realm of What Is Hidden

---

1. The Alter Rebbe is Reb Schneur Zalman of Liadi (1745), one of the great Hasidic masters and author of the *Tanya*.

INFORMATION

THE APPARENT REALM OF WHAT IS APPARENT

The Apparent Realm of What Is Apparent is the dimension where things are obvious and concrete, where one single unknown is hidden amid an enormous amount of information. Because there is so little dark in the midst of so much light, everything seems to point obviously to an apparent result. It is as if time could be reduced to a given instant and space, to a given point. The universe is frozen, static, allowing us to predict and to infer. In this dimension, logic has absolute mastery and efficacy.

Yet a constant danger haunts the realm of the concrete and obvious: that we will forget that the Apparent Realm of What Is Apparent is a reduction. In other words, because it is so easy for the human mind to fathom this realm, we may be confused into expecting that everything can be reduced to its boundaries. Those who do not see have no knowledge of what they do not see; those who do see, by contrast, think that what they see is all there is to see. Hence the expression "They have mouths but cannot speak; they have eyes but cannot see; they have ears but cannot hear" (Psalms 135:16–17).[2]

---

2. Translation from *Tanakh: A New Translation of the Holy Scriptures According to the Traditional Hebrew Text* (Philadelphia: Jewish Publication Society, 1985).

Sight is at one and the same time a resource and a limitation, but this is hard for us to perceive. When elementary school children are presented with a math problem, its givens are stated in reduced form, as part of an exercise in training logical thinking. For example: "A boy went out and bought six apples. When he got home he had only two. How many did he lose on the way?" Plausible answers include "none," "three," "six," and "two." How so?

"None," because his apples were in fact stolen. "Three," because he ate some on the way. "Six," because the apples were spoiled and couldn't be eaten. "Two," because the boy got the apples at fifty percent discount. "None," because apples aren't lost, they've been recycled.

The logically acceptable answer is clearly "four." Yet this could be considered the least informative answer, and therefore the worst. The answer "two," on the other hand, is existential in nature and rich in information. If the boy received a fifty percent discount, it is as if he had lost only two. Not only is this sound accounting; it also tells us something about human nature and how we deal with loss.

We often find ourselves thinking along similar lines. For example, we lose some money and then immediately remind ourselves we've just made a big profit elsewhere. So we count our losses as the first amount subtracted from the second. This is not absolute truth, but it is our existential truth.

When we cling to literal readings of reality, we cannot gain insight beyond the original proposition, either by introducing other aspects of reality (the fact that the boy got a discount), by questioning (were the apples lost, eaten, or stolen?), or by interpreting (apples are not lost but recycled). Life, however, is forever demanding that our interpretations move beyond the literal so that we may better understand and deal with the world around us. The Apparent Realm of What Is Apparent is nevertheless vitally important. One of the great masters of Jewish tradition, Rashi,[3] dedicated his whole life to the study of the literal as a kind of art. In his wisdom, he knew the tremendous impact that could be caused by answering "four" to this simple math problem—and thus viewing literalism not as the whole of reality but as part of it. The Yiddish proverb "Be careful! If you keep going that way, you'll probably get there!" is not a redundant statement of the obvious. To understand the full significance of the literal, we must recognize that it does not exist in isolation. It is merely a component of reality, formulated within a void that renders its meaning comfortable to us. Rashi knew this. He knew that the literal dimension can reveal much about other dimensions of experience. But if these are to be revealed, the literalist must always be aware of the background or frame that lends meaning to the literal.

The literalist who examines propositions profoundly but who trains his or her perception to understand them solely and always in direct relation to what they purposefully leave unsaid is truly a wise person.

This is the trained eye of the literal Kabbalist. For this person, the text or proposition is written in black fire, but the emptiness around the letters—in white fire—is just as real and created with just as much purpose and sophistication.

In order to discern the most subtle and complex levels of the universe, we must let ourselves be surprised by the simple and the concrete. This surprise is what allows us to take a fresh look, from the angle of what is hidden. Once the surrounding areas of ignorance have been uncovered, we will see in a whole new light what at first appeared unformed and limited.

The Apparent Realm of What Is Apparent is actually the point of connection with the Hidden Realm of What Is Hidden. Like the horizon that joins earth and sky, the Apparent Realm of What Is Apparent is as far as the naked eye can see. At that

---

3. "Rashi" is an acronym for Rabbi Shlomo ben Isaac (1040–1105).

intersection where the obvious seems to touch the sublime, the ground does not literally touch the heights. If you reach the place where your eyes thought the earth was kissing the sky, you will find the same distance between them as from any other place. It is precisely by getting some distance and understanding the fundamental blind spots that surround knowledge—I call them "ignorances"—that the scientist can measure the curvature of the earth on the horizon—or the Kabbalist can find connections between things that never meet.

When it comes to discovering our ignorances, the Apparent Realm of What Is Apparent is the essential human tool.

Text and Context

Historians, biographers, and literary critics share a long-standing concern: the search for primary sources and data in their original form and essence. With their purpose of achieving a deeper understanding of a given subject, these specialists depend on originals in their rawest, most literal form. The fewer additions or deletions a document has suffered over the course of time, the more valuable it is. A literal text can shed light on spheres of interpretation or ways of identifying the ignorances surrounding any given affirmation. It is the mapping out of ignorances that enables us to lend meaning to an affirmation, complementing our knowledge.

The Bible as a text provides the ultimate example of this kind of relationship to knowledge. Revelation is an ongoing interaction between a text and its interpretations. Though many might disagree, interpretations can actually influence the literalness of a text. What we must do is define a dimension where the Apparent Realm of What Is Apparent can express itself fully, untainted by ignorances—that is, what is hidden—which render it less readable and hamper the process of understanding and resolution.

The Apparent Realm of What Is Apparent must be clearly delineated and separated out. It is through this realm that human beings may experience the most hidden dimensions of what is hidden. Our first and foremost task thus becomes *defining the basic text of a given document, thought, or situational context.* Revelation is made possible through this identification of the concrete, objective text, in conjunction with a thorough awareness of its volatile nature.

If a text or context is captured in its solid form but its volatile nature is ignored, we interrupt the sacred process of creating fragments of meaning amid surrounding ignorances. A solely objective reading of a text or proposition transforms it into a mere extension of this ignorance. Working with nothingness and voids requires the utmost caution, so that what has gained form does not return to the void. That this happens easily is evinced by how hard it is for us to solve problems. The Kabbalist's secret lies in preserving the original text so that through it he or she may reveal the hidden side of what is apparent within it, or the apparent side of what is hidden within it, or even the hidden side of what is hidden within it. Kabbalists protect themselves from madness (from the void) by remaining in steady contact with the Apparent Realm of What Is Apparent. It is only possible to travel extraordinary paths over a firm ground-text. According to the poet and philosopher Jacques Derrida, "For Jews—and for poets—the book is bound within itself, endlessly self-reflexive; its own content is its own representation. The Jew's and the poet's house is the text: they are wanderers born only from the book. . . . Amid the fragments of the Broken Tablets, the poem grows and the right of speech takes root. Once again the adventure of the text begins like a weed, like the illegal alien far from the 'motherland of the Jews,' which is a 'sacred text surrounded by commentaries.' "

For these "illegal" interpretations to emerge, the fundamental prerequisite is total fidelity to literality. Illegal interpretations make it possible to gain an understanding that surpasses the Apparent Realm of What Is Apparent, without ever losing contact with this dimension of literality.

Let us consider the question "What is the most important quality for a writer to have?" "A small appetite," a yiddishe kop might respond, in utmost faithfulness to the literalness of the question, which seeks to ascertain the most practical attribute for someone wishing to become a writer. Although other answers would inarguably be just as correct, this one pinpoints a prerequisite that is not sufficient in itself but that is surely indispensable for anyone wanting to pursue such a career. It is an answer that takes into account a broader reality, which does not exclude the issue of survival from the original question's realm of interest. It runs counter to conventional thinking, which would immediately supply an answer from among a list of literary talents. What we must understand here is that this is not the field of interpretation but of literality. This answer does not suggest any other reality for the condition "writer," does not alter the original inquiry regarding "what is needed," and does not ignore the notion of "quality." It is absolutely faithful to literality.

The Question of Vessels

The realm of the literal is essential because it says something— and when something is said, all the world's mysteries are defined by what is left unsaid. Based on the Bible, the Jewish liturgy says "God spoke and the world came into being."[4] Creation is the act of asserting something and through that act fashioning

---

4. In the introductory prayers (*pesukei de-zimra*) before the Psalms in the morning service.

everything that was *not* asserted. This is the cosmogony of the Lurianic Kabbalah, according to which God made room within Himself so that the Whole could be empty and of such a nature that when anything is asserted, the Whole is implied. Only thus are awareness and knowing possible.

Creation, the primeval origin of everything, is a process of differentiation and the formation of "vessels" to allow forms to come into being. Light and the pure essence of Wholeness could not be contained in any vessel without instantly shattering it. The breaking of vessels is what constituted the act of Creation, which therefore is an expression not of essence but of form. Even when shattered, form is what allows essence to be contained. The most amazing thing in the history of the universe is the way essence was able to make room for form. The history of vessels unfolded: forms began to hold essence. Essence does not reveal the world around us; form does. The vessel "car" defines and expresses an absolute essence in the same way the vessel "dog" or "mosquito" does. All the essences we know are derived from the forms around us. We fly thanks to the vessel "air," the vessel "bird," and all other vessels that permit us to understand the laws governing the flight of heavier-than-air objects. The problem we face daily is to generate more forms out of what we have learned from forms themselves. Solar energy, for example—which could solve all of our planet's energy problems—is waiting for vessels capable of holding it. When the first form appeared, all other possible forms were defined. The Apparent Realm of What Is Apparent is precisely this dimension of vessels surrounded by everything they do not contain. This is the value of a text or proposition: it is a form that allows other forms to exist and, at the same time, defines essence by exclusion. This is why the Ten Commandments prohibit the making of images: forms give us access to something formerly beyond our reach and mislead us, for forms exist precisely where God made Himself absent.

What they affirm is part of an ongoing relationship with what they do not affirm, and only what they do not affirm is truly worthy of worship. All is form; only God is essence.

Knowledge is derived from forms and produced through the creation of forms. A good text must have "form"; its literality is essential to generating knowledge about its ignorances and about what is not said. To assure a text its literal form, not allowing it to be defiled by interpretations, is to prevent essence from replacing form again and prevent Creation from reverting to its original state, devoid of vessels.

The function of consciousness and knowledge is to produce vessels, not to shatter them as the heretic does, seeking essence when form is fundamental and thus interrupting a constructive process transpiring in a territory purposefully at a remove from the essence.

A story is told about a famous Hasidic rabbi on his deathbed. All around him, in the next room and outside the house, hundreds of disciples gather to hear his parting message. Finally, his most devoted student summons up the courage to go up to him and whisper, "Rebbe, don't leave us without a last word of wisdom; we are all here waiting for a word from you."

For a while there is no reaction, and many disciples start weeping, fearing that their beloved master has departed. Suddenly, however, his lips begin to move and, with great difficulty, he whispers something. The student draws closer and hears the words, "Life is like a glass of tea."

The other disciples standing around the bed hear the wise words repeated by the student and grow very excited. "The Rebbe says life is like a glass of tea," they tell each other. The statement is quickly relayed to the front room and from there to the streets, where people enthusiastically repeat to one another, "The Rebbe says life is like a glass of tea." Everyone is greatly perplexed by such a mystical revelation, until somebody dares to ask, "*Why* is life like a glass of tea?"

Gradually everybody starts asking the same thing, and the

question travels back from the street to the front room and from there to the bedroom where the Rebbe lies dying. Again, his closest disciple musters up his courage and asks, "Honored Rebbe, we beg you to tell us: why is life like a glass of tea?"

With his last breath, the Rebbe shrugs and whispers, "All right, so it's *not* like a glass of tea."

The question that returned from the streets had the power to revert an answer back into a question. Whenever questions address essences, form should be most welcome as an instrument of response. A good answer depends on the ability to distinguish between question and answer, and this distinction is not as simple as you might think.

A question often carries within it more elements of an answer than an answer itself, while answers may carry more elements of a question than the question itself.

In our story, the Rebbe stated a proposition that could have been preserved at the level of meaning, thereby breeding numerous commentaries—perhaps even whole books—regarding its hidden significance. Because the students did not accept the Rebbe's statement as a "text," it was returned to meaningless.

The emptiness of the statement becomes apparent when the masses, influenced by the person who "reverts" answers into questions (i.e., the heretic), obliterate the context surrounding the answer. The point is not only to analyze the Rebbe's words but to understand the information that places them in context— such as "deathbed," "message," "Rebbe," and "disciple"—so that what in isolation does not constitute an answer can, in this specific context, be understood as one.

Just as the person who does not revert answers into questions is a hero of meaning, so is the one who formulates questions, as we will see shortly.

What Is an Answer?

One of the characteristics of the stereotypical Jew is that he or she always answers a question with another question. In a well-known anecdote, somebody asks a Jew, "Why do you people always answer a question with another question?" To which the Jew promptly replies, "Why not?"

A question can lend new depth to another question and, as in the anecdote, answer it. A question is already part of the process of elucidation, and the literalist knows this. Those who work with "texts" know very well that producing a list of questions, even if you don't necessarily find the answers to them, is one method of interpretation. Interestingly, in the ancient rabbinical academies, literalists like Rashi focused chiefly on the effort to understand not possible *answers* but the *questions* that may be extracted from a text. In doing so, literalists legitimize a text by conferring on it an absolute meaning, while likewise delineating the text and thereby lending form to the void surrounding it.

Jews have acquired fame as literalists and as specialists in form. This might seem contradictory, as a basic tenet of the Jewish faith prohibits the worship of forms. Yet at the same time that the literalist knows he must never lose sight of the essence, he also knows that his labor is carried out in the realm of convention. This is what allows him to capture that most elusive of things: meaning.

A Hasidic tale that takes its inspiration from the East may help us understand this more clearly:

A man tormented by doubts about the nature of truth decided to travel to a distant village to find a rabbi known far and wide for his wisdom. It was a long and tiring journey, but he finally arrived and immediately started making inquiries about seeing the famous sage. The villagers scoffed: "The Rebbe has been in retreat for nearly twenty years and you, a perfect stranger, think you can see him just like that?"

But the seeker wouldn't give up. He waited until the Rebbe's closest disciples were distracted and managed to slip into the room where the old man was studying. After a while the Rebbe looked up. "Excuse me, venerable Rebbe; I have come from far away with a question that has long been troubling me. I am hoping that, in your great wisdom, you can give me an answer."

"And what is the question?" asked the Rebbe affably.

"What is the essence of truth?" the visitor responded. The Rebbe looked him deep in the eyes, got up, and slapped him.

Shocked and upset, the man went to a tavern to try to drown his disillusion in drink. A local lad, noticing his heavy drinking, asked what was wrong. On hearing the story, the young fellow pondered, "You know, the Rebbe wouldn't do a thing like that without a reason. There must be an explanation."

From a nearby table, one of the Rebbe's disciples, who had been listening in, intervened: "The Rebbe slapped you so you would learn never to trade a good question for an answer."

An essential part of any pursuit is knowing how to be a literalist. This means you cannot distance yourself from questions but must stay within their orbit, taking advantage of all they can do toward clarifying and reclaiming meaning. It's as if we had gone back to that TV quiz show, where the contestant makes decisions inside a closed booth that prevents him from understanding just what kind of deal he has struck. Answering is an action that, if not performed cautiously, can further darkness and ignorance; it can trade what is most important for that which is most superfluous, with an arrogance and a certainty that are even more obscuring than ignorance itself.

This is why one of the safest ways of reacting to a question is by asking another question. Knowing how to ask this question so as to enrich the first question without falling into redundancy is a difficult challenge requiring keen wisdom.

The next time you are faced with a puzzling question, just ask yourself more and more questions. This is a way of drawing out the apparent side of what is apparent. Form will thus become so well defined in all its clarity and with all its nuances and outlines that it will reveal essence itself.

The process of acquiring knowledge demands that we refuse to see until what we see adds rather than subtracts.

Pockets of Mental Resistance

A disciple told Reb Bunam that he had become a coachman. The rabbi replied: "Your head will now be occupied with horses; so it seems you have turned your mind into a stable."

Our mind sees, hears, and understands depending on how we format it. No dimension suffers more from our predispositions and prejudices than literality. It is as difficult to keep from incorporating affirmations and texts into our routine thinking patterns as it is to break deeply ingrained habits of behavior. Just as we often need therapy to change our behavior patterns, we only break free of our mind-sets when we discover that they are the greatest source of ignorance and therefore work through them. Even a naive or irrational person may be less ignorant than those who perceive reality through the distortion of their conditionings.

According to an old Yiddish saying: "A watch that has stopped is better than one that is fast or slow—at least it's right twice a day!"

If you are bound to certain patterns of thinking, you will never see reality, texts, or propositions with clarity. In this case, you are better off not even seeking answers. The terra firma of the text—which will later be abandoned by the interpreter—must first be very well defined. Otherwise you cannot be a wanderer or a pilgrim of meaning, for you will have nowhere to return to, and the concepts "home" and "exile" both lose their power to enrich meaning. It is in the constant movement from certainty to estrangement that we can find meaning. The feeling of comfort gained from being at home and the feeling of wonder associated with being in exile are both fundamental to a sense of purpose.

When conditionings are legitimized, it is as if everything were in movement but with no reference points.

Rebbe Nachman of Bratslav offers a fascinating commentary on the following excerpt from the Talmud: "When Solomon married Pharaoh's daughter [1 Kings 3], the angel Gabriel came down from heaven and stuck a reed into the ocean. Refuse from the ocean attached itself to the reed, and eventually land was formed. On that land, the city of Rome was founded. Later on, the Romans destroyed the Holy Temple" (*Shabbat* 56b; *Sanhedrin* 21b).

Rebbe Nachman offers this interpretation of the story:[5] If we internalize a form of wisdom that is foreign to the spirit of true wisdom, we create mental blocks. Solomon represents wisdom. Pharaoh's daughter represents slavery and patterns of conditioning (as a metaphor, being in "Egypt" is generally associated with addiction and dependence). The marriage to the Pharaoh's daughter therefore symbolizes the wedding of potential true wisdom (Solomon) to biased and compromised (slavery) wisdom. The mind itself is the ocean. Mental blocks to true wisdom are represented by Gabriel's descent to earth to "stick a reed in the ocean." The resulting refuse offers fertile ground for the founding of Rome, which is the bias that invades and takes over, destroying any chance of reaching the Holy Temple—that is, of arriving at meaning.

True deprogramming of the mind makes room for literality and the construction of a "primary text." Unless we can empty our minds in this fashion, we cannot create vessels capable of holding knowledge. The pseudo-vessels created by "reeds" stuck in our thoughts are not resilient but fragile, for they mix form and essence in one single unit. True vessels, on the other hand, are made of pure form.

The mind, just like the Almighty, has to make room inside

---

5. Adapted from Rebbe Nachman, *The Candelabrum* (Jerusalem: Breslov Research Institute), p. 57.

itself in order to create and be creative. Otherwise it
temple after temple, returning everything to a state of mea...
lessness. To be able to work with form, you must accept it in its
raw state, without trying to trim its edges or fill its voids. Your
mind must tend as little as possible toward manipulating or dis-
torting propositions. Each marriage of a new quest with the conditionings left from old quests hinders your seeing and
understanding—and destroys temples erected to hold sacred
wisdom.

Aesthetic Mental Blocks

Not everyone is satisfied with his looks,
but everyone is satisfied with his mind.

—*Yiddish saying*

We are prisoners of our minds to such an extent that rarely are
we dissatisfied with them. One of the figures most often caricatur-
ized in Jewish literary tradition is the "genius," best defined as
someone who is seduced by the beauty of his own mind. So perfectly conceived and so naturally suited to his every thought does
his mind appear to him that he cannot understand why the outside world has so much trouble recognizing his talents and his
outstanding aesthetic sensibility. Such people remain lost in the
labyrinths of their own philosophies, always finding ways out and
answers that in fact afford neither a way out nor an answer.

To avoid this pitfall, we must know how to be ignorant. Learning to recognize the "nonaesthetic" areas of our minds—that is,
those areas where established patterns do not rule—is a fundamental stage in the process of acquiring knowledge. We will only
overcome certain obstacles on the path to solutions if we invest
in our ignorances rather than endeavoring to maximize our cer-
tainties. A good researcher is the one who knows how to use the

trash can appropriately. She knows when to focus on her ignorance, rather than wasting time with her depleted knowledge.

The teacher asks: "How would you divide eleven apples equally among twelve children?"

The nonaesthetic answer would be: "Simple. Make applesauce."

Doubting our own aesthetic responses is healthy; it helps us make the most of life. Here is where literalists play an important role. When they delineate and underscore what is stated in a given text or proposition, they reveal what was not said and give us access to ignorances. People who work with symbolism, metaphors, or allegories often have less clarity about surrounding ignorances. With their taste for aesthetic structures, they are much more likely to spot the contradictions, incoherence, excesses, or omissions in texts and propositions.

The genius's most common, and most serious, mistake is to develop a self-centered logic that has little or nothing to do with the outside world. The genius believes that knowledge is static and that it suffices for him to choose the most aesthetic, most automatic options from within his own mind—and the universe will adjust to them. The following Jewish tale is a good example:

Shapiro had had a very good year, so he decided to take a cruise to France for the first time in his life.

The first night, he was shown to his place for dinner and found himself sharing a table with a well-dressed Frenchman. When Shapiro arrived, the Frenchman rose, bowed, and declared, "Bon appétit!"

Shapiro replied, "Shapiro!"

The same ritual took place at every meal. On the last day of the trip, Shapiro happened to run into the purser, who informed him: " 'Bon appétit' is not his name; that's just French for 'I wish you a hearty appetite.' "

"Is that so?" said Shapiro. He couldn't wait to rectify the situation. That evening at dinner, before his companion could do a thing, Shapiro stood up, bowed ceremoniously, and declared: "Bon appétit!"

Whereupon the Frenchman rose and replied, "Shapiro!"

The ease with which Mr. Shapiro falls prey to his own preconception regarding the nature of the exchange with his new friend is a measure of the problem he has dealing with his own ignorance. His first understanding goes unquestioned, and apparently he does not check to see whether there are any alternative meanings for *bon appétit*. But he grows even more ridiculous when, after having discovered the meaning of the expression, he assumes that his logic does not interact with the outside world's. In interpreting reality, Shapiro created a text. When he discovered that reality was different, he changed his interpretation but held on to the same text. Similar scenes happen every day when spouses, employees and employers, friends, and relatives attempt to communicate with each other.

Know how to remain open to the entire range of possibilities contained in a proposition or a text. Be a literalist, enumerating all the realities compatible with what you don't know. By checking your ignorances, you might not necessarily understand what someone else is saying, but you can avoid erecting further obstacles to communication. Should you catch yourself in an erroneous reading of reality, deal with your mistake as an intrinsic part of a new reality.

Valuing Ignorance

Awareness of ignorance is fundamental in any type of research. The failure to maximize our powers of thinking is in great part fed by the conditionings and anxieties that human nature creates. To our detriment, we are easily diverted from our goals without realizing it. That is why mapping out our ignorances can be an effort-saving strategy.

When Isidor Rabi, the 1944 Nobel Prize winner in physics, was interviewed about his achievements, he said he owed it all to his mother. "When we got out of school, all the mothers would ask their children what they had learned that day. My mother would inquire instead, 'What did you ask today in class?' " The basic difference between a successful and an unsuccessful student is that the former tries to understand a problem within the entire surrounding context, while the latter fixates on the problem itself. If any parameter is changed on a test, the second student won't be able to solve the problem.

Exploring the question of mental productivity, the rabbis asked their disciples: "Which is better, a fast horse or a slow horse?" The answer? "It all depends on whether you're headed in the right direction or not." At first it seems obvious that a fast horse is better, since the notion of "horse" leads us to think in terms of getting somewhere, and this leads us to think of efficiency, or speed. The rabbis were trying to provoke just such a conditioned response in order to make their disciples realize that any question contains ignorances and that identifying these ignorances is essential to answering the question. Shadows help define contours. On a wrong road, a slow horse is better, since less backtracking will be needed once the mistake has been discovered. A proposition can point us toward an answer, but on our way to it we must work hard to uncover all possible and relevant unknowns.

Even though these unknowns may initially be perceived as obstacles to knowledge, they serve to shed light on more effective forms of answers. If we don't know the right way, being aware of the risks involved in taking a fast horse allows us to concentrate on our search to find the right path as quickly as possible.

The Baal Shem Tov, the founder of Hasidism, synthesized this notion in the following tale:

A devout man came to the Baal Shem Tov with a complaint: "I've made an enormous effort to serve the Lord sincerely and honestly, but I haven't noticed any change or improvement. I'm still the same ordinary, ignorant person as before."

The Baal Shem Tov answered: "You've realized you are ordinary and ignorant, and that in itself is a great accomplishment."

This facet of the Apparent Realm of What Is Apparent can greatly enhance our understanding of the Hidden Realm. It is no wonder that the Hidden Realm of What Is Hidden adjoins the Apparent Realm of What Is Apparent precisely where the latter's ignorance lies. Anyone who wants to learn from the obvious must consider what the obvious can teach us about what is not obvious. Unfortunately, we are most often seduced by the aesthetic appeal of the obvious, and we absorb it with an illusory sense of superiority. We love clarity because we feel powerful and secure in it; but true wisdom lies in the intimidating perception of darknesses.

Nothing arouses perception of darkness as effectively as the light of the obvious. Take this to heart.

Pathologies of Obviousness

While the Apparent Realm of What Is Apparent serves a functional purpose, one should not rely on it alone in the struggle to survive. Competition is fierce in this dimension. Everyone thinks the same, goes to the same places, tries the same things, and has the same ideas when they are in the domain of the Apparent Realm of What Is Apparent. Going full circle from proposition to resolution of a deeper issue demands exploration of the distinct realities of the apparent and hidden realms.

A story from Jewish mystical tradition reflects the profound relationship between other realms and the Apparent Realm of What Is Apparent—specifically, between literality and "hiddenness." It is the story of the four sages who entered Pardes. *Pardes*, which literally means "orchard," is said to be the origin of the word *paradise*. Moreover, the term *pardes* is formed by the initial letters of the four forms of interpretation in Jewish tradition: *P*, the first letter of *peshat*, which refers to literality; *R*, the first letter of *remez*, which represents allusive, metonymic interpretation; *D*, for *derash*, metaphoric and symbolic interpretation; and *S*, for *sod* ("secret"), mythic and mystical interpretation.

The legend tells how four sages entered the orchard but only one managed to come out unscathed, while the second died, the third went crazy, and the fourth became a heretic.

If we look at this journey into the orchard as symbolizing the act of thinking, we can draw some interesting analogies. The sage who returns unscathed is someone who can voyage through the Hidden Realm of What Is Apparent, the Apparent Realm of What Is Hidden, and the Hidden Realm of What Is Hidden, confident he will reemerge in the Apparent Realm of What Is Apparent without any harm to his ability to function. This person successfully harvests the fruits of this dense orchard and transports them into a realm where they may be enjoyed. What is obvious, or apparent, may be recovered as terra firma in the midst of the instability and fluidity of these other worlds.

The journey of the sage who lost his life represents complete disconnection among the object of inquiry, the original question, and the answers obtained. An irreversible rupture occurs between the logic of the original problem and the production of knowledge, resulting in a complete disintegration of the Apparent Realm of What Is Apparent. There is no way left to communicate answers in any concrete or logical manner, making it impossible to return—nothing can be learned from this journey. In this case, Pardes does not yield up further knowledge. It is the opposite of coming out of the orchard unscathed—where "unscathed" represents a state of potential increase in knowledge, either because more information or a greater awareness of ignorances has been achieved. If we wish to relate this to possible pathologies, we could say the journey resulting in death represents exposure to excessive doses of *sod* (secret), where the Hidden Realm of What Is Hidden thwarts any attempt to find answers. Darkness invades the clarity of the obvious.

The journey that ends in madness represents an exaggerated emphasis on *derash* (metaphor/symbolism). Here the answers generated by the visit to the orchard might even touch on the original question, but they are not applicable. These answers remain stuck at the level of the Hidden Realm of What Is Apparent, producing absurdities that become insurmountable obstacles to their practicability. This dimension of madness has a distorted relationship to the Apparent Realm of What Is Apparent. It gathers inedible fruit from the orchard—answers that do not answer.

The man who returned from the journey as a heretic fell victim to intoxication by *remez* (the allusive/metonymic form of interpretation). He let himself be treacherously seduced by the Apparent Realm of What Is Hidden. As we will see later, this realm can lead us to make inappropriate links between areas of doubt and areas of answer. The apparent aspect of the Apparent Realm of What Is Hidden comes to be viewed as tantamount to the Apparent Realm of What Is Apparent—and this apparent aspect is assumed to be the answer. Allusions derived from the process of thinking (that is, the journey through the orchard) replace the original question, and much as the resultant answer may even be an answer, it is an answer to a different question. So the heretic, unlike the madman or the dead man, comes back with an answer but doesn't catch on to the fact that it comes attached to the wrong question. If we believe that an answer fits a specific question when in fact it doesn't quite fit, our whole thinking process is jeopardized. The heretic gathers edible fruit, but it has grown rotten. Having failed to convert the molecular composition of this fruit into objective reality, he nevertheless brings it out of the orchard in mutant form.

The pathologies that appear in the Apparent Realm of What Is Apparent—and that so often hamper our ability to think effectively—have to do with nonapplicable theories (leading to death), permanent deviations from objectivity (leading to madness), and internalized mistakes (leading to heresy).

The worlds that interact within Pardes are dangerous because if any one of them takes precedence over the others, no fruit can be harvested. But it must be emphasized that the Apparent Realm of What Is Apparent offers the same sort of risks as the other realms. If you are a prisoner of the obvious—that is, a "simpleton"—you will certainly end up experiencing a bit of all the other pathologies (death, madness, heresy) because in failing to fully understand reality, you will cast a light that blinds rather than illuminates.

It is important to realize when we engage in a serious quest for an answer—when we visit the Pardes of thought—that we are engaging in an interactive process. Answers are not to be found in this or that apparent or hidden realm but in their interconnecting passageways. Successful journeys into the orchard involve free access to all of these dimensions and will yield the fruit-answer best suited to a given question at a given moment.

UNDERSTANDING

THE HIDDEN REALM OF WHAT IS APPARENT

When a guest coughs, it means he's missing a spoon.

—Yiddish proverb

The Hidden Realm of What Is Apparent is a dimension of what is apparent, or of consciousness itself. This "hiddenness" merely reflects the fact that what is apparent has been covered up by something likewise apparent. I am not suggesting that this realm cannot be classified as obvious—it is simply that what is obvious has been hidden. When we discover something hidden within what is apparent, it is usually a startling experience: "Why didn't I ever notice that before?" Parables and stories often serve as tools in this task of unveiling apparent information, concepts, or situations that at some given point are hidden.

The prime feature of this dimension is that it accentuates the apparent. In other words, what is apparent would not be so apparent were it not for this partnership with its hidden realm.

In Jewish interpretive tradition and thought, a concept may appear in two distinct states: *mashal* (signifier) and *nimshal* (signified). To illustrate, we can say that water is in the hidden form of the apparent when it is solid—that is, when it is ice. Ice can be seen as *nimshal* and water as its *mashal*. Water reveals certain properties and characteristics of ice that are more evident in the form of water than in the form of ice.

In terms of mental analysis, this is tantamount to asking what something is like. Nothing is ever as clearly what it is as when we can say it is like something else. The signifier is therefore that which we liken to the signified. We do this even more naturally in the case of differences. We find it easier to say something differs from something else, because differences have to do with the Apparent Realm of What Is Apparent. Tall/short, fat/thin, good/bad, dry/wet, big/little—these are clear-cut. Just as with similarities, when we examine differences there is a reciprocal relation between signified and signifier: "tall" is easier to understand when compared to "short," the meaning of "fat" becomes sharper when linked to its signifier "thin," and vice versa. Similarity, however, contains within itself a hidden order of approximation that is never the same as the oppositions found within differences. Of course, not all differences constitute opposites, as when "similarly different" things are not "wholly different" but rather part of the reality of the Hidden Realm of What Is Apparent; as such, these similarly different things are open to interpretations within the realm of metaphor and symbolism. And this is all obvious—it is the nature of Creation that all things are different from all other things but that no two things are identically the same, unless they actually *are* the same. So we see that similarity is always a likening of one thing to another, which provides access to nuances not found in absolute identity, or in absolutely opposite identity.

We more easily recognize when something is similar to something else than when it is different from something else.

Within the Hidden Realm of What Is Apparent, the signifier does not define the signified but reveals modes and ways of thinking about it and understanding it better. Since the act of unveiling similarities has the effect of triggering these ways of thinking, it is similarities that reveal this hiddenness in what is apparent. To exemplify, let us look at some relationships between *mashal* and *nimshal*, taken from David Freedman's story "Mendel Marantz":

> What is rent? A fine for being poor.
>
> What is money? A disease we like to catch but not to spread.
>
> What is pessimism? A match that burns the hand.
>
> What is optimism? A candle that lights our way.
>
> What is a woman? A lightning bolt—beautiful and radiant until it strikes you on the head.
>
> What is like love? Butter: it's only good with bread.[6]

When these signifieds are linked to their signifiers—rent/fine, money/disease, pessimism/match, optimism/candle, woman/lightning, love/butter—they gain clarity because we have opened up a gamut of ways of thinking about them and understanding them. This means that "finding something else like it" is a way of attaining knowledge. Rent is not a fine, but insofar as rent can be *likened* to a fine, we discover more about its nature.

We always have something to learn through this method of extracting *mashal* from *nimshal*. The search for similarities is thus a fundamental tool in research and cognition. At the age of two, my son used to say, "It looks like it but it's not. . . ." This statement lent concreteness to things he encountered in the Hidden Realm of What Is Apparent. In likening one thing to another while affirming that the two things were not identical, he was learning about the world. So everything can teach us about everything else, as long as a relationship of similarity can be found.

---

6. Nathan Ausubel, *A Treasury of Jewish Humor* (New York: M. Evans & Co., 1988).

According to a Hasidic tale, a rabbi from Saragossa said:

"We can learn something from everything that exists in this world!"

"What can we learn from a train?" challenged one disciple.

"That because of one second, we can lose everything."

"And from a telegraph?"

"That every word counts, and we can be charged for each one."

"And the telephone?"

"That what we say here is heard There."

We could go on with other examples: the bicycle—as in life, we can't stop pedaling; the radio—if you're tuned to one station, you can't be tuned to another; the fax machine—there's no communication until someone else gives the signal. And the microwave—among other things, it's best to keep spirituality on low heat: certain shortcuts can burn your soul on the outside but leave it cold inside.

Solutions to be found within the hiddenness of what is apparent are expressed in similarities. If *that which is* is what matters within the reality of the Apparent Realm of What Is Apparent, what matters here is *that which is like*. Likening one thing to another explains more than the rigidity of a static conclusion contained within an objective reply. This hiddenness is endowed with the dynamics of *that which is "something like"*—because whatever is "something like" is unfinished and continually reveals infinite nuances of possible answers. Herein lies an efficacity that expresses itself more in conceptual and formative terms than in practical ones.

Reframing

Reframing is another way of asking, "What is this like?" But here the emphasis is on separating a given text from the context in which it is presented. Interpreting a proposition or understanding a situation from another angle is a way of identifying what something is really like, without detours or distortions.

When a loss occurs, for example, it is very common in the Jewish tradition to use this reframing technique to find comfort and learn acceptance. When something unfortunate but of minor importance happens—for example, if a cup or a plate breaks—the conditioned response in a Jewish household is *"Mazel tov,"* which means "What good fortune!" The situation has been reframed to say: "It's a good thing something worthless broke; now you've been made aware that you're preoccupied, and you can be more careful so that no more serious accident will happen." If we look at it this way, losing money, scraping a tire against the curb, and countless other situations that many other people would take as signs of bad luck can be reframed as signs of good luck. Most certainly this was a lesson learned from the hardships that have marked the history of the Jewish people down through the ages. It is survivor knowledge, as evinced in this reframing: "It's better for a Jew to lose his beard than for a beard to lose its Jew."

Reframing is vital in problem solving because it exposes hidden elements of what is obvious. Let us consider the situation narrated in this traditional Jewish anecdote:

A young man who worked in his father's shop caught an employee stealing. He went to his father, told him the story, and asked: "What should we do with the fellow?"

"Give him a raise," his father replied in a blink.

"A raise?" his son asked in astonishment.

"If he was stealing, it means he's not earning enough," the father explained.

The son was expecting his father to suggest some form of punishment, not a reward. But his father's understanding of the situation—which may not be appropriate to every situation involving theft—probably reflected a very sensitive view of reality. By reframing the event, a good employee kept his job and saw his inadequate salary raised. The son had been seduced by the aesthetics of logic, which demanded some form of punishment. If we don't know about reframing, our choices are reduced to a single plane of possibility: from among all types of punishment, which should be applied?

Not binding yourself to one sole context constitutes a kind of perspicacity that derives from an acquired awareness of the ignorances and uncertainties inherent in our store of knowledge. A perverse sultan corners the surviving Jew and says, "If you state a truth, you will be put to death by hanging; if you state a lie, you will be decapitated!" The Jew replies, "I am going to die decapitated." He has saved himself by checkmating the sultan: if the Jew died decapitated, he would have stated a truth—and thus should have been hanged; if he wasn't decapitated, he would have stated a lie—and thus should have been decapitated.

What is apparent has led to error. We must find other ways of dealing with the apparent, in which the hidden elements of what is apparent can become manifest.

If you are to master the Hidden Realm of What Is Apparent, your mind must remain malleable, not locked into the rigors of a literal text, even though based on this text. You must listen to propositions from a critical distance so that the aesthetics of logic do not expropriate your power to perceive.

A story tells us that the Rabbi of Berdichev saw a man running down the street without so much as glancing right or left.

"Why are you running like that?" he asked the man.

"I'm running after my daily bread, Rabbi," the man replied.

"And how do you know that your daily bread is not running after you? It might be right behind you, and all you need to do to find it is stay still a bit, instead of running nonstop."

The rabbi has played with the very image created by the man in the story—that of running after his daily bread. We see that the rabbi is wise to the Hidden Realm of What Is Apparent because he hasn't overlooked the need to appropriately frame what is happening. His focus on a particular aspect of the man's behavior—the failure to look either left or right—makes it immediately apparent that this man is not "present." It is such "presence" that constitutes opportunity—and what is opportunity here? Daily bread!

Both this example and the story of the employee who stole from the store illustrate how much the Hidden Realm of What Is Apparent can have direct consequences in the practical world. But this realm can make another type of contribution as well, insofar as practical problem solving is always linked to the Apparent Realm of What Is Apparent. The Hidden Realm of What Is Apparent sheds light on the spot where we stand when asking the question. All other realms, except the Apparent Realm of What Is Apparent, are stages within the realm of research and laborious study. Conquering an understanding of a problem during these stages does not suffice to solve the problem, but it does shed so much light on the area surrounding it that the problem becomes easy prey to solutions lying within the Apparent Realm of What Is Apparent. Consider this Hasidic story:

Rabbi Yechiel Mikhal lived in absolute poverty, but joy was always with him. One time someone asked him, "Rabbi, how can you pray, day after day, 'Blessed art Thou, Who sees to all my needs,' if you have none of what a human being needs?"

The rabbi answered him, "What I most likely need is poverty, and that is what I have been provided with all these years."

The rabbi's situation has been totally reframed, transforming poverty into something a person may need. "Poverty" acquires a positive potential. Just as ignorance in conjunction with information forms knowledge, need in conjunction with that which is provided forms our subsistence. Maybe satisfaction, much like knowledge, is not an absolute measure but a condition of comfort that has been acquired through an awareness of need, lending relevance to that which is provided. But that is philosophy, and what interests us here is methodology.

Rabbi Yechiel's statement is important not for what it says about resignation or theology but because it manifests a certain wariness concerning any attempt to direct a person's reasoning. Even the measure of our needs—which to us seem to be one of the most concrete elements in our universe—is in fact a concept devised by the human mind.

Reframing is a subversive way of approaching reality. It is generally an uprising against unanimity or consensus. Walter Lippman used to say, "When everyone thinks alike, no one's thinking." Reframing is above all a sign that something is going on in the orchard. It recognizes that "truths" can be impostors and that thought processes are fraudulent and easily corrupted, that the act of thinking entails not only an intellectual dimension but emotional and affective dimensions as well.

Can't or Don't Want To?

Among the various methods of reframing, some are paradigmatic. Central to the experience of human reasoning is the reframing approach, which suspects that any inability to understand is the result of an insufficient desire to understand. The Hasidic masters constantly employed this concept. When their disciples displayed incredulity or difficulty in following certain lines of reasoning, the masters would ask, "You *can't* understand, or you don't *want* to?"

Inarguably this is one of the main mental blocks within the emotional realm, or the Hidden Realm of What Is Apparent. Each of us has a vested interest in particular ways of acting and thinking, ways that have become so entrenched and have such well-organized lobbies to defend a given approach to understanding life that it is almost impossible to break free from them.

When we say, "I can't," we are not weighing an intellectual impossibility but an emotional one. "I can't" means "I don't want to."

During the Cold War, Russian Jews used to say: "If you corner a Russian and demand his opinion, he'll reply, 'Of course I have an opinion. But I don't agree with it.' "

When it comes to the Hidden Realm of What Is Apparent, discovery and revelation are only possible when the Self can overcome the ego and all of its commitments. Catharses, which are often a form of reframing a situation, constitute a kind of successful negotiation, where the ego makes commitments to the greater Self within each of us.

Every individual should learn how to foster and strengthen this inner "opposition" to the tyranny of our minor comforts and interests. Feeling at ease or being able to flirt with something we don't believe and don't like means opening a window into the Hidden Realm of What Is Apparent.

When operating within the Hidden Realm of What Is Apparent, we map out surrounding ignorances. If within the Apparent Realm of What Is Apparent, ignorance is anything not explained by a given system of logic, then within this emotional dimension, ignorance is everything that is imposed in order to preserve a given model of emotional balance. Learning how to survey these political commitments that determine how reality should be understood is a way of gaining wisdom. It allows us not only to penetrate our own armor but that of others as well—allowing us to understand others not only from the angle of what they say and do but also from the angle of what they don't say and don't do, as we will see later when discussing the issue of "transparency."

We should perhaps strive to make our Self more a judge than a sage. Its task is not simply to judge facts but mainly to verify the integrity of the witnesses and of the proposals submitted for judgment. Judging is just one step in the long process of check-

ing the consistency of the underlying facts upon which an understanding or decision will be based.

Reframing amounts to putting two witnesses face to face and
building a case from the perspective of each party's interest in
masking the truth. These interests reveal hidden agendas that
better account for reality. By bringing them up to the surface, by
making them apparent, we can understand why certain tenden-
cies emerge.

A Hasidic story about the methodology of thinking provides
us with a metaphor for this process of identifying ignorances—
or, better put, of identifying how coarse and ignorant we are when
it comes to understanding that which we have no interest in understanding:

> One time a rabbi was watching as a trapeze artist balanced
> on a tightrope. When the performer was through with his act,
> the rabbi asked him, "What is the secret to not losing your
> balance?"
>
> The tightrope walker in turn inquired, "Where do you
> think you should look to keep your balance?"
>
> The rabbi replied, "Certainly neither at the ground nor at
> the rope."
>
> "Correct," the performer said. "You have to keep looking
> at the poles at the end of the rope. And when is the most
> dangerous moment?"
>
> The rabbi answered, "The moment when you have to turn
> around and you lose your reference point for a second."
>
> "Precisely," the performer agreed.

The act of thinking cannot be jeopardized by the immediacy
of the next step. Making sure that your very next step will be the
right one is like looking down at the rope. You risk the longer
walk, which should always be tied to a goal, to the pole at the
end of the rope. Any researcher will tell you that the moments
when you turn around—when you are left without a pole to guide

you—are key to keeping your balance and therefore to successfully completing your process of inquiry.

The moments when we take another step along the rope reflect
the Apparent Realm of What Is Apparent. The moments when
we look toward the pole—which allow us to reframe each step—
reflect access to the Hidden Realm of What Is Apparent. But
those brief instants when we are left without our guide poles,
those turning points, belong to a very different reality: the reality
of what is hidden, be it the Apparent Realm of What Is Hidden
or the Hidden Realm of What Is Hidden, as we will see later.

Crossing the tightrope of thought without losing your balance
and falling means you must cast aside minor, more immediate
interests concerning your next step in favor of a bigger goal, the
goal of successfully completing the crossing.

Transparency

If you know how to understand what is *not* said within that which
is said, if you know how to ask whether "cannot" does not in fact
mean "don't want to," and if you can reframe situations, then
you can penetrate the countless layers covering reality. Among
other things, you will gain the ability to see beyond the dissembling we human beings so often engage in, and instead will catch
sight of a transparency that is at once surprising and frightening.

There is a famous story about a Hasidic rabbi who had the
power to read what was going on inside a person's soul just by
looking at his or her forehead. When this rabbi went to visit a
certain city one time, the people there all wore hats to cover their
foreheads, fearing the rabbi's powers. When he reached the
town, the rabbi said, "Fools! If I can see inside your heads, is
there any way a hat could keep me from doing so?"

The truth is, we don't realize how transparent we are. We
think we can disguise and dissemble our feelings through our

actions or reactions, and we fail to understand that they are evaluated on the outside through a broad gamut of signals that leave them naked to the eye. It is not at all unusual for us to practice mental contortionism, offering explanations and justifications in an effort to prove something while we are in fact proving just the opposite. The harder we try to cover up reality, the more boldly and clearly it stands out. This transparency stems from our conveying a large quantity of information through a "reversed signal," allowing observers access to ever more explicit information that belies the sincerity of what they see on the surface. We can all use this knowledge to help understand reality when it manifests itself in the hidden form of the apparent—dissembled yet nevertheless evident.

The act of making a person transparent can be a way of drawing an individual closer. If we do this without making the person's act of dissembling look ridiculous, but by forging more sincere ties between people, the dissembler will perceive this "unmasking" as a manifestation of a kind of captivating intelligence. The following story can help us analyze this process:

> When he was still quite young, Mikhal, Rabbi of Zlotchov, sought out the Baal Shem Tov (also known as the Besht) because he wanted to discover whether he should become the great mystic's disciple.
>
> One time the Besht took Mikhal along on a trip. After driving the cart for some time, it became clear that they were on the wrong road. "What's happening, Rabbi?" asked Mikhal. "Don't you know the way?"
>
> The Besht replied, "It will be made known to me at the right time."
>
> And they took another road, which likewise proved to be wrong. Mikhal asked, "So, Rabbi, have you gotten lost again?"
>
> "It is written," said the Besht, as calm as can be, "that God will realize the desire of those who serve Him sincerely.

And thus He is realizing His desire to have an opportunity to laugh at me."

The words touched young Mikhal deeply, and without further questioning himself, with his whole soul he accepted the Besht as his master.

The rabbis never liked to miss an opportunity to engage in an encounter with insincerity, knowing that insincerity has great potential as a teaching tool. They knew that insofar as this act of unmasking reveals certain hidden sides of what is apparent, it enhances the thinking process. When someone's fraud is denounced, it silences the one who is insincere, because it exposes the entangled thought networks and structures destructively bound up with "not knowing."

In their judgments and interventions, the rabbis made constant use of "transparency techniques" to awaken wisdom. By disclosing what was hidden within certain outer appearances, they opened new paths toward personal growth. The next two examples illustrate how transparency can be applied to solving practical problems.

A certain man of highly questionable conduct went to the Rabbi of Ropshitz to confess his sins and atone for the error of his ways. On the one hand he was extremely embarrassed to recount all his misdeeds and misfortunes to the just rabbi; yet on the other he knew he had to list every one if he hoped to find a way of atoning for them.

The man decided to tell the rabbi that it was one of his friends who had committed these deeds, but was so ashamed to narrate them personally that the friend had assigned this task to him. He would listen to the rabbi's advice and convey it to his friend.

With a smile, the rabbi told the fellow, who was watching him with curious and cunning eyes, "Your friend is a fool. He could very well have come here to see me himself and pretended to be representing someone else who was ashamed of coming to confess personally."

With great tact the rabbi has reframed reality so the man in the tale can see himself from the outside. He has been denuded before his own eyes, made transparent, so he can now not only understand how feeble were his ploys but also recognize that they differ in no wise from the errors for which he wishes to atone.

On his way to town a poor farmer came upon a wallet in the road. Looking through it, he found ninety dollars, a name and address, and a note stating: "If found, please return this wallet. Ten dollars reward." The farmer quickly searched out the address and returned the wallet to its owner. But rather than showing gratitude, the owner said, "I see you have already removed the ten dollars due you as your reward."

The poor man swore he had not; the owner insisted that ten dollars was missing from the total of one hundred dollars that had been in his wallet. So they took their tale to the local rabbi, who listened patiently to the farmer and then to the owner of the wallet.

"Whom will you believe, Rabbi?" challenged the rich man. "That ignorant farmer or me?"

"You, of course," answered the rabbi, much to the farmer's chagrin.

But then the rabbi took the wallet and handed it over to the farmer. Now it was the owner's turn to be astonished: "What are you doing?"

"You said your wallet contained one hundred dollars. This man says the wallet he found contained only ninety. Therefore this wallet can't be yours," said the rabbi with finality.

"But what about my lost money?" cried the indignant man.

Patiently the rabbi explained: "We must wait until someone finds a wallet with one hundred dollars in it."

Once again, the rabbi perceived what was really happening thanks to transparency. It was the owner of the wallet himself who made evident the solution to the problem. He was the one who wanted to set the conditions for everything, and especially for reality itself. So be it. Let reality be understood in his terms but taken to its ultimate consequences. Within the world of absurdity or the realm of hiddenness, remaining on the path of madness or of distorted perspectives may reveal unexpected resolutions or logic.

When you have no reason to doubt anyone's word, it is interesting to observe what version of reality will gain form. It is a version that responds to no one's specific interests, for it is false—and in some fashion it will also strike back at whoever spreads falsehoods. The rabbi's line of reasoning reflects the notion that you cannot deal in misrepresentations of reality without running into fallout. And this kind of conclusion is the product of access to transparency.

In neither of these two cases did the rabbis argue with the versions that were presented. Able to understand reality through transparency, they knew how to maneuver within the realm of different versions in order to arrive at a solution appropriate to reality itself and not to one version of it alone.

Paradoxical Interventions

What's the heaviest thing in the world?
An empty pocket.

—*Yiddish proverb*

Paradoxes can also be used to shed light on areas of ignorances. These proposed responses reverberate within us mentally until they eventually trigger insight into an issue. They can be either redundant in nature or contradictory. The following two examples illustrate paradoxes in their redundant form:

> Once while playing one of his regular hands of cards with a friend, Morris got into an argument and spurted out in anger, "What kind of person can you be, if you sit down to play cards every day with a guy who sits down to play cards with a guy like you?"

> Groucho Marx sent a telegram to a club in Hollywood that had invited him to join: "Please accept my refusal. I don't want to belong to any club that would accept me as a member."

In the first case, the use of redundancy reveals how much mistrust and lack of character are hidden within the two men's interaction. As soon as one of the players cheats, the other one unveils the Hidden Realm of What Is Apparent. The redundant paradox renders a sharper understanding of the apparent nature of their interaction.

In the second case, Groucho wanted to voice his disapproval of snobbish clubs that employ bias in selecting their members. Through his refusal within the hidden realm of appearances, Groucho cleverly plants a resounding doubt in the minds of the club members: "He doesn't wish to belong to the club because he doesn't deserve to; but if we have chosen him and we deem him worthy of membership, why wouldn't he join a club where he could be a member? Does this mean he refuses to belong to a club whose members meet our standards?"

Without igniting a polemic, Groucho has gotten his point across. His sophisticated reply leaves no room for members to feel offended, although the club has undoubtedly been criticized. Paradoxical interventions lead to efficacious solutions within the realm of irony and criticism.

Another example has been handed down from Hasidic tradition:

> Whenever Rabbi Menachem wrote a letter from Israel, he would always sign it: "He who is truly humble."
>
> Someone once asked the Rabbi of Rizin, "If Rabbi Menachem was so humble, how could he refer to himself that way?"
>
> "He was so humble," replied the Rabbi of Rizin, "and his humility was so internalized, that he no longer considered it a virtue."

Here a redundant paradox serves to illuminate the true essence of the word *humble*. This rabbi is so humble that he can refer to himself as such since the notion of humility is meaningless to a truly humble person. The rabbi's provocative decision to so entitle himself was intended to broaden our understanding of this particular human quality. Through that which is apparent—which is contradictory—Rabbi Menachem opens the possibility of absorbing its hidden realm. This hidden realm—a man so humble that humility is meaningless to him—makes it apparent what humility is really all about.

The other type of paradoxical intervention is a contradiction where a logical opposite sheds greater light on a situation or a question. Let us look at two examples:

> One member of a congregation exclaimed to another: "Our rabbi is such a good person and lives so frugally on his paltry income!"
>
> "That's true," observed the other. "In fact, he'd probably starve to death if he didn't fast every Monday and Thursday."

The second person has used a paradoxical intervention to lend greater clarity to what his friend has said. If the rabbi did not have an inner, spiritual life to sustain him, he could not get by on the pittance he earns. The fact that his fasting constitutes an "interruption" of an inadequate daily diet is absurd, but at the same time it probably offers him some relief, allowing the poor man to bear up under these living conditions. Understanding is achieved by relying on an element of paradox, which reveals the hidden realm of an apparent situation.

> An eighty-two-year-old woman tottered into Dr. Neyrowitz's office. "Doctor," she told her physician, "I'm not feeling too good."
>
> "I'm sorry, Mrs. Kupnick, some things not even modern medicine can cure. I can't make you any younger, you know."
>
> Mrs. Kupnick retorted, "Doctor, who asked you to make me younger? All I want is that you should make me older!"

The physician misinterprets reality, and his insensitivity leads him to conclude that the woman is asking for the impossible. After the woman gives her adamant reply, what first appeared to have been a witty comment is proven foolish. After all, as a professional it is up to the physician to help the woman, not issue a judgment concerning the destiny of nature or the woman's personal situation. Through her paradoxical intervention, the woman reveals the true understanding of her request that lies behind the misunderstanding. By using a logical opposite to reframe the situation, the doctor has been put in his place as an active subject and has been forced to realize that the only thing ridiculous about the situation is the brash—and mistaken—way in which he perceived reality. Much more than a mere reply, a paradoxical intervention serves as a biting critique of certain behaviors, as it reverberates through our thoughts.

Irony

Irony can also disclose the world hidden within what is apparent. Irony is a way of stepping back from immediate reality to observe

it at a remove so that we may respond to it in a witty and tren-
chant manner. As with other methods for revealing the Hidden
Realm of What Is Apparent, irony exaggerates a devious reading
of reality in order to unmask that which is apparent. Irony often
appears in the form of a paradox, satirizing a preposterous proposition and taking it to extremes. The proponent of the sorry idea
is forced to realize his or her lack of good sense. Irony does
not conclude; it merely induces by highlighting foolishness or
inappropriate behavior.

A slight tension is left hanging in the air whenever irony is
expressed, because the person expressing the irony does not
"kill off" his or her prey (that is, the target of irony), and this
means that irony also has a reverberating effect.

> A farmer went to a rabbi and complained, "Rabbi, we're suf-
> fering the worst drought in years. My fields aren't producing,
> my cattle are dying, and now my family is sick from starva-
> tion. What should I do?"
> "Don't worry," the rabbi said in a soothing tone. "God
> will provide."
> "Yes, of course, I know," the farmer agreed. "I'd just like
> Him to provide until He starts providing!"

The irony does not contradict the rabbi's words. Yet the sense
of urgency, the sense of absolute reality experienced by someone
whose family is in need, strikes us more forcefully through its
contrast with the rabbi's commonplace. The farmer skillfully and
diplomatically lets the rabbi know that he hasn't understood the
nature of the poor man's visit. Above all else, if the rabbi has no
solution to the farmer's problem, he should at least know enough
to refrain from supplying any answer rather than delivering a
non-answer.

Within the universe of responses, sages have long seen this
as a fundamental question. "All my days I have been raised

among the sages, and I have found nothing better for oneself than silence" (*Pirkei Avot* 1:17). This statement refers to an active answer. Silence should not be construed as a non-answer like the rabbi's but as one possible reaction attuned to the farmer's question. It is, however, very hard to offer silence as an answer. Silence as a response is peculiar to the very wise.

One of the richest topics within Jewish folklore's legacy of irony is business. Just as one of the favorite settings for Jewish tales is "So-and-So went to the rabbi and said . . . ," exchanges between merchant and customer are also a bountiful source of meaningful human interactions. Indeed, many problems that erupt on the psychoanalyst's couch are also reproduced when a counter stands between two individuals. Here are some examples:

> Sadie Weintraub went into the bakery and asked for two rolls.
> "Forty cents, please," said the baker.
> "Forty?" Sadie exclaimed. "What? Twenty cents a roll? Your competitor across the street only charges twelve cents!"
> "So buy them from him," said the baker with a shrug.
> "But he's all out of rolls."
> "Lady, when I'm out of rolls, I only charge five cents each."

This paradoxical intervention is not simply a reply to the customer. It also reveals secrets of the complex world of business and competition. It's easy to keep prices down when you have nothing to sell. The storekeeper has poked fun at a client who thinks she is demonstrating consumer awareness. There is a huge difference between a customer who does know his or her rights and is willing to protect them and one who wants to reveal what is obvious: that the merchant is enjoying a profit. By answering as he does, the baker shows the customer how little she knows about the marketplace. A customer should never propose that he or she gain advantage over the merchant—otherwise, each will have to step to the other side of the counter. The client's proposition often drives the businessperson to the point of madness, to the point of wanting to say, "You haven't figured out what your role in this game is—I sell and make a profit; you go away with merchandise that costs its value plus my profit." Of course we can question the percentage of profit earned in this "game" but not the concept of profit in itself—which is often what a disgruntled customer tries to do.

A good merchant knows his or her role, and knows full well that the customer can be fooled. A Buddhist monk tells how his exchange with a Jewish shopkeeper in New York taught him a valuable lesson in life. The monk was looking at a computer in a glass case when he heard someone say in a noncommittal tone: "Don't buy that one. The other one's better." The monk saw that the businessman was addressing him while he went about other matters. "Why is the other one better?" inquired the monk. "Well, I can see you don't understand computers. You're looking right at the worst products. If I wanted to fool you, it'd be easy. You don't need to know why this one is better precisely because I could cheat you. You should trust my words. This one's better."

This paradoxical interaction—"I can fool you, so trust me"—allows us to understand that for a certain type of judgment or answer to be appropriate, it doesn't necessarily have to give us absolute control over a given situation. You can have sense enough to recognize the reality of this interaction and, accordingly, to place your stakes on what seems most evident, even though it is hidden by the "uncertainty" of non-control. It is not a matter of intuition but of making a conscious decision that, owing to a non-obvious reality, it is obvious what the right thing to do is. Based on a feeling, this interpretation of what is real is solidly grounded in a careful evaluation of reality.

One very hot day Mr. Finkelstein went into a shop to buy a paper fan. "What kind of fans do you have?" he asked.

"We have five-cent fans, twenty-cent fans, and fifty-cent fans," the shopkeeper replied.

"Give me a five-cent fan," said Mr. Finkelstein.

"OK," said the shopkeeper as he handed him a thin Japanese fan.

Ten minutes later, Finkelstein was back. "Look at this piece of junk you sold me!" he roared. "It already broke!"

"It broke?" the shopkeeper said in surprise. "And just how did you use it?"

"How did I use it? How do you use any fan? I held it with my hand and waved it in front of my face. Isn't that how you do it?"

"No, no," the shopkeeper explained. "With a five-cent fan, you have to hold it quite still and shake your head back and forth in front of it."

The shopkeeper pokes fun at the customer because the customer doesn't know how to interpret reality correctly. It was up to him to ascertain he was buying inferior merchandise, because the price was cheap. The shopkeeper had to point out that five-cent fans don't work the way Finkelstein had imagined. By underlining this distinction, irony speaks the customer's language. "It's not the material that's of poor quality; you don't know how to use what you bought." The problem—as the shopkeeper makes clear—is the customer, not the merchandise.

Predictions

Predictions are another way of revealing the Hidden Realm of What Is Apparent. Predictions are really prognoses born of a capacity to read reality with utmost clarity and sensitivity. Someone who sees what others can't manages to describe things in a way that others find supernatural. There are two types of predictions: hidden obviousness and chains of obviousness.

Hidden obviousness:

Hitler was having nightmares, so he told his orderlies to find someone to interpret his dreams.

"Ah!" the soothsayer proclaimed, "I see that you will die on a Jewish holiday."

Hitler was frightened yet curious. "What holiday?" he asked.

"Whatever day you die will be a Jewish holiday."

Chains of obviousness:

Mr. Rosen had spent two weeks in New York on business and was taking the train back to his suburban town. Sitting next to him on the train was a young man he didn't know. Since the train ride was long, Mr. Rosen decided to strike up a conversation.

"Where are you headed?" he asked.

The stranger smiled and said, "To Glens Falls."

Mr. Rosen was surprised. "Why, that's where I'm going! As a matter of fact, I live there! Is it a business trip?

"No," said the young man. "It's social."

"Oh, do you have relatives there?"

"No, I don't."

Mr. Rosen thought a bit. "Are you married?" he asked.

"No, I'm not."

Now Rosen mused to himself. "He's going to Glens Falls, he's not married, it's not business, and he has no relatives there. So why is he going? Obviously, to meet a girl—to meet her family? Confirm their engagement? But whom? There are only three Jewish families he could possibly know . . . the Resnicks, the Feldsteins, and the Sanowitzes.

"It couldn't be the Resnicks. Resnick has only sons. The Feldsteins have two girls, but one's married, and the other's in college and she wouldn't be home at this time of year. It must be the Sanowitzes. They have three: Marsha, Rebecca, and Rochelle. Marsha is already engaged. Becky is too unattractive for this nice-looking young man. So it must be Rochelle. Yes, Rochelle! She's beautiful!"

With this, Mr. Rosen broke his silence and smiled at the stranger. "Well, congratulations on your forthcoming marriage to Rochelle Sanowitz!"

"But—but how did you know?" stammered the young man.

"Why, it's obvious!" answered Mr. Rosen.

It is not hard to travel the world of the Hidden Realm of What Is Apparent as long as you have an imagination, and—*because* you have one—you know that reality appears before us reproduced in different versions. If we consider the propositions lying before us as versions, as texts that have been deliberately chosen from among all possible texts, we can disassemble and assemble reality. This is a world where we discover that there is no discontinuity between a proposition and the person who devises it, nor between the situation and where that person is within his or her life at that particular time.

What has not been said is said. What has not been done is done. What has not been given is a given. You can tell the voyager of the hidden realm from the voyager of the apparent realm by these shadows of words, deeds, and givens.

WISDOM

THE APPARENT REALM OF WHAT IS HIDDEN

A complete fool is better than half a wise man.

—*Yiddish saying*

In entering the realm of the hidden, we are delving into a kind of thinking that differs substantially from what we have analyzed so far. The apparent world—whether the Apparent Realm of What Is Apparent or the Hidden Realm of What Is Apparent— can be apprehended and grasped; we come to know it through our consciousness. It is a world of definite, distinguishable forms, where light and clarity allow us to see and to perceive. The world of hiddenness is not as well differentiated. Edges and borders blend into each other here, even though forms still exist—but they are more fluid forms that at one moment display the outlines of other forms and at another moment emerge as part of these same forms. Like the interlinking images and structures of our dreams, these forms take shape and then dissipate in themselves. This is the world we call the subconscious, where fragments of form make it possible to momentarily grasp forms that manifest themselves and then immediately retreat into hiding. This is the place where forgetting and remembering seem to be one and the same experience, where no border lies between knowing and not knowing—where the two merge and allow us access to what it would seem impossible for any vessel of our cognition to contain. But that is not quite the case.

The ability to perceive still works in these worlds, and that is why they are part of the "orchard" of thought. They represent knowledge branded with confident affirmation of what was seen and perceived for only a few moments—knowledge apprehended from images preserved on our retinas and in our cells, even after the impinging object of cognition is no longer present.

The world of myth makes a classic distinction between the realms of appearances and of hiddenness. That which is apparent is represented by earth, and in the perception of the animal kingdom, earth's prime characteristic is the fact that it can be discerned. A creature that climbs a hill and looks off toward the plains will clearly see the different forms present there. Animals, trees, birds, rocks, streams, and so on are all distinguishable. The eye makes out and apprehends the forms. The hidden world is represented by water, or more precisely, by the sea. When we look at the ocean we cannot distinguish the countless creatures and forms contained within. What we see is a fluid whole, the collective of something that is brimming with pieces and portions. We cannot see its shapes without viewing the sea as a whole. Moreover, these shapes cannot survive outside their medium, infinitely denser than the air enveloping the Earth—while on land, forms are infinitely denser than the medium enveloping them.

What clouds our view of the hidden world is the trouble we have separating a form from its medium. It is in fact impossible to understand a form without understanding its medium, to understand a text without its context. This strange world holds secrets within it that may manifest themselves in the apparent world without ever gaining the concreteness that imparts a sense of clarity.

The characteristics of this hidden world startle and surprise us. We can tame the impossible within this territory; indeed, much of what we recognize as impossible within the apparent realm is nothing more than a manifestation of what is hidden.

The history of the Jewish people offers a particularly enlightening illustration, one that speaks of the impossible and how these kinds of questions can be solved. The Bible tells us the Israelites left Egypt to flee slavery. But they hadn't gone very far when they found themselves besieged by the mighty troops of the Pharaoh, who had reneged on his decision to free them. They were trapped between very concrete (apparent) forces that could carry them back to their old world—that is, they were trapped between the most powerful army of the most powerful civilization of their day and the most concrete obstacle limiting terrestrial species: the sea. There was no way out. The proposition confronting them called for a solution not feasible within the territory of land, of the apparent. The solution would be to turn to the sea, to traverse its fluidity in a crossing nothing less than fantastic.

The willful determination of this people came near to reaching its limits when they realized they had exhausted any chance of finding a way out via the land routes of rational reasoning and of logic, routes that would permit them to escape between the hosts of Egyptians troops and their chariots—and so they began paying court to areas of the impossible. Casting themselves into the sea, the waters were miraculously divided. And the Israelites went into the sea upon dry ground: a wondrous crossing became possible.

The Israelites had cast themselves into the hidden world of fluid knowledge; they had penetrated the depths of the subconscious and succeeded in fording it to reach new banks, in a new land—unscathed. Rashly attempting the same crossing—but with no awareness that they were stepping into the sphere of the impossible, and furthermore lacking any deep understanding of the reasons behind this crossing—the Egyptians found out just how suffocating formlessness can be. The Israelites could make out "form" because they recognized the medium surrounding it and thus arrived at a sense that set them on firm ground. Charged with a mission bereft of any greater content and that had nothing of the transformational about it, the poor Egyptians found themselves mired in quicksand. Their means of conveyance through this world—their chariots, horses, and concreteness—were so ill suited for the dimension into which they ventured that it entrapped them. The seas closed over them and robbed them of the differentiation afforded by land—and they were swallowed up like forms of the sea-medium. On the far bank, the Israelites celebrated their mastery over the impossible; they had discovered how much the hiddenness of the sea could serve as a tool for understanding and coping with reality. For them, the waters became waters of renewal and transcendence.

In specific terms, when we approach the world of the Apparent Realm of What Is Hidden—part of which lies within the realm of hiddenness—we are penetrating the territory of intuition. This world discloses readings of reality that may manifest themselves to us quite clearly but not without our first traversing threatening swamps of shapeless forms. Someone looking on from the world of appearances cannot follow this process. Although this person may stand in awe of what the process can achieve within the realm of the concrete, practical world, he or she lacks the tools for understanding it.

We saw earlier that one way of solving problems more efficaciously is to confront ignorances. What is the difference between two students who get respective grades of 0 and 100 on a math test? If their IQs are the same, we must conclude that this tremendous difference in test performance has to do with their ability to map out ignorances. The student who got a zero absorbed information on how to solve a specific problem explained by the teacher on the blackboard but failed to understand the principles implicit to its solution. If only a slight change is made in the proposition, the student will not know how to solve it and will score zero. This is how information (the Apparent Realm of What Is Apparent) and understanding (the Hidden Realm of What Is Apparent) differ in their efficacity.

In the world of wisdom (the Apparent Realm of What Is Hidden), it is not enough to merely map out what you don't know; you must make greater use of what you don't know than of what you do know. While attending a conference on Intuition and Management, I heard a lecturer argue that "we use a mere ten percent of our brains; imagine if we used one hundred percent." I responded by saying that this would be a disaster in terms of our efficacy, for we depend greatly on the void within our minds to carry out important processes whose end results are resolution and survival.

What often happens in life is that the student who scored 100 on the test does not go on to be a shining star of success in adulthood, while the one who got a zero becomes a success in business. This is what becomes possible when someone manages to move from the plane of appearances to the plane of hiddenness.

There is a Jewish anecdote that exemplifies this:

Mo was a terrible student, while his cousin Danny was top in his class. But when they grew up, everything Mo touched turned to gold, while Danny didn't make much of himself. When Mo won the lottery, Danny simply couldn't stand it any longer. Beside himself, he went to his cousin, determined to get to the bottom of it all: "This time you're going to tell me how you do it! On top of everything else, how did you manage to win the lottery?"

Mo replied, "Well, if you really want to know, I'll tell you. The night before I bought the ticket, I had a dream. A choir of angels was singing sweetly, and there were seven rows with eight singers in each one. There was no question about it: the

next day I went out and bought a ticket that ended with the
number sixty-three. That's all there was to it!"

"But Mo, eight times seven makes fifty-six, not sixty-
three!"

"Oh, really? OK, Danny, so you're still the one who knows
all about math!" Mo concluded.

Danny cannot understand that there are areas of life where
"the void" offers the solution. Faulty calculations notwithstand-
ing, in this arena Mo is more efficient than Daniel, who believes
that you can explore intuition by relying on the faculties of reasoning alone.

The world of hiddenness is unquestionably a strange territory
where the absurd is a vital link between types of logic that at
first may strike us as unrelated. It is a world where a complete
fool is better equipped than half a sage; where naiveté and foolishness can reveal unexpected aspects of knowledge. It is a
brand of knowledge that is little concerned with solving problems
and that often derives from the astuteness of producing a new
good question for every answer.

There are no manuals to this world; the hidden realm is made
accessible first through experience, and only then as perception. The Maggid of Kozhenitz made this clear to a woman who
came to ask him to pray for her because she was unable to bear
children.

"My mother had the same problem as you," the Maggid told
her. "Then one day she came across a wonder-working rabbi
and brought him a gift of a coat. I was born the next year."

"Thank you very much," said the woman with a radiant
smile. "I will do as your mother did. I will give a great rabbi
a coat."

The Maggid smiled. "Don't bother, because it won't do
any good for you. You see, my mother had never heard this
story!"

Aiming at the Real Target

We are in the allusive world now. Rather than asking ourselves what something looks like, here we allow ourselves to draw associations like "This reminds me of that." Certain topics, objects, narratives, or environments allude to others and weave a chain of forms all wrapped in an ethereal medium, in a field of perception. If "mountains" represent "strength" on the plane of appearances, then on the plane of hiddenness they might easily be related to "Mondays." The connection between one thing and the other is not evident but is steeped in a wealth of knowledge. As the most common way of studying and intervening in this realm, psychotherapy has demonstrated the tight bonds between this world and concrete reality.

But how can we "handle" this world and take advantage of it as a factory of knowledge?

The first step is learning that within this world we can only arrive at knowledge through reversal: that is, by linking good questions to our answers. Each answer unfolds into countless possible good questions, which in turn constitute pure and useful cognitive material. These answers often do not yield clarity, and whoever attempts to unveil them as answers will become as dangerously mired as the Egyptians. What in fact provides "answers" and releases perceivable manifestations within the apparent world are the questions created by these answers.

The following story helps us understand the principle of reversibility, and its utility:

A hunter venturing into the woods came across some targets painted on different trees. He was surprised to see that all the arrows had hit the bull's-eyes. He was so curious to meet the perfect marksman who had accomplished this that he searched far and wide. Finally he found the archer and questioned him about his feats:

"What is the secret behind your accurate aim? How can an archer attain such perfection?"

"It's quite simple," replied the archer. "First I shoot my arrows, and then I paint the target."

This describes the method of reversibility. Each arrow shot hits the target right on the bull's-eye. Identifying the bull's-eye only after shooting the arrow might not exactly be a demonstration of skilled marksmanship, but it has much to teach the archer about his shooting. It is obvious that this method will not improve anyone's aim. Even if we rationalize by saying that painting the target after the fact may indeed be a lesson if the archer measures how far off he was from the targeted point, we are still within the realm of the apparent—that is, in the territory of the Hidden Realm of What Is Apparent, of ignorances that enlighten, but not in the territory of the Apparent Realm of What Is Hidden. The hidden realm cannot be translated into the apparent realm. And the reverse route—a target that reveals a different aim—is what becomes important to "knowledge." In other words, a new question is revealed by the answers found through processes of association and allusion.

Psychoanalysis, for example, concerns itself with this other question. Its knowledge comes from recovering the true question, the one that hits the bull's-eye, in contrast with the original question, which has no direct link to the target that was hit.

In the Apparent Realm of What Is Hidden, the true target is the one created after the arrow has been released. In what seems to be an absurd inversion, it is the target that seeks the arrow, and not the other way around. By definition, in the world of subconscious thought, the origin of the inquiry does not matter; the thought existed prior to the question itself. So curiosity comes after knowledge. In this sense the process of "thinking" is reversed.

What is incredible about the realm of hiddenness is that it

knows (has the answer) beforehand, for its nature has to do with essences. This explains why the answer is irrelevant in the shaping of forms. It is, rather, the question that is an element within the universe of form. It is the question that represents the specific within the collective of possible answers (targets); answers become "sea"—they are an integral whole that cannot be taken apart and that serves as a medium.

In order to take advantage of this medium that is so dense that it obscures specificities, the marksman cannot rely on the skill of "control." Anyone who controls knows what targets are to be hit and would mock the hunter who paints targets after the fact. But this hunter harvests information from life's experiences to which the controller has no access. A prisoner of the world of forms and of logic, the controller believes that anything that is not "controllable," that cannot be produced in a laboratory, does not convey knowledge.

Painting targets after the fact means recognizing relations between cause and effect where the effect produces the cause. This is what the rabbis had to say about a very important dimension built into the fabric of the text of the Torah. This sense of simultaneousness reflects a much greater interest in processes than in pat answers. Processes are answers in a dynamic state. Because of their mobility, the answers are perceived solely through the new questions. Yet it is not a relationship of derivation but of allusion.

Different Brands of Logic

Another characteristic of the intuitive world is that it is multifaceted. The philosopher Martin Buber suggested that the story of Adam and Eve eating the forbidden fruit, whereupon "the eyes of both of them were opened" (Genesis 3:7), is a reference to this specific aspect of hiddenness. Their eyes were opened to the contradictions and ambiguities inherent to all things. The expression "knowledge of good and evil" (Genesis 2:17), according to Buber, refers not to an acquired consciousness of moral categories, but to an acquired access to the tension between the contradictory propositions that exist in all Creation. This awareness of the contradictory nature of reality is quite painful, and God had benevolently attempted to protect human beings from it. But from the eating of the apple to this day, men and women have been condemned to perceiving the ambiguities of reality.

A Jewish anecdote portrays this question quite brilliantly:

> Two Jews sought out a rabbi to settle a dispute. Arriving at the rabbi's house, they found him studying, while his wife sat in a corner of the room. The rabbi inquired, "What is your complaint?"
>
> The first plaintiff laid out his argument in convincing fashion, to which the rabbi reacted, "So *you* are right!" Then the rabbi turned to the second plaintiff: "And what do you have to say for yourself?"
>
> The second plaintiff offered an equally eloquent argument. "So *you* are right," responded the rabbi.
>
> Listening to their conversation, the rabbi's wife broke in: "My dear husband, may you live to be one hundred and twenty years, but for heaven's sake, how can they both be right?"
>
> Stroking his beard, the rabbi concluded: "*You* are right, too!"

From the angle of the apparent realm, it seems as if the rabbi, holder of wisdom, has gone crazy. Richard Raskin argues that this anecdote can be perceived as fitting into one of three categories: "role-fiasco," "tactical maneuver," or "exemplary deviance."[7] In the first case, we can say that the rabbi displays an

---

7. Richard Raskin, *Life Is Like a Glass of Tea: Studies of Classic Jewish Jokes* (Oakville, Conn.: David Brown Book Co. [Aarhus Univ. Press], 1992).

"absurd" kind of wisdom, a caricature. If perceived from the second perspective, the rabbi's wisdom has failed to yield any answer but has proved itself instead to be a strategy for avoiding conflict not only with his wife but also with the two plaintiffs. Looked at from the third angle, the rabbi deliberately wants us to realize that the norms of logic simply do not account for the whole of human possibilities.

These three possibilities can be seen as representing three different worlds. From the perspective of the Apparent Realm of What Is Apparent, the rabbi's reaction is a "role-fiasco." Two plaintiffs seek out a rabbi and receive an exasperating answer. Looking at it from the Hidden Realm of What Is Apparent, the rabbi seems to have his own agenda. The original issue is reframed in such a way that the rabbi is not worried about settling the affair by issuing a final verdict but first and foremost wants to protect himself by dealing with all parties diplomatically. The third case takes us to the Apparent Realm of What Is Hidden—in other words, it is obvious and inarguable that the rabbi wants to ratify the possibility that "this one is right," "this one is right," and "this one is right." Legitimizing the knowledge that is contained within ambiguity and in different brands of logic, this teaching is exemplary of this more evident side of what is hidden.

A number of branches of science have recently presented new response theories as part of an effort to create models that account for reality. One theory argues that there are different ways of "being right."[8] The ability to legitimize these various "rights" is valuable as a tool in attaining knowledge. Raskin demonstrates this graphically using reversible images[9] often known as Gestalt figures, which can be perceived in different ways: for example, the Rubin image (fig. 1), the Schuster trident (fig. 2), and the Necker cube (fig. 3).

---

8. Raskin, p. 30.
9. Raskin, pp. 27 and 31.

FIGURE 1. The Rubin image

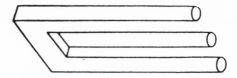

FIGURE 2. The Schuster trident

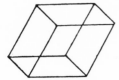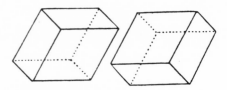

FIGURE 3. The Necker cube

Reversibility represents perception of the Apparent Realm of What Is Hidden, because it builds forms that then disappear. Solution-finding may mimic this process. Often we can only apprehend certain kinds of knowledge if it gains a reversible form. Form exists, but solely within its medium, which perpetually is replacing it with another form. One depends upon the other but is not defined by the other, unlike the realm of the apparent. Here again, what is hidden is dynamic and cannot be grasped like something static. It responds in movement and for this reason links into other questions.

Intervening in the Intuitive World

One of the most common human dreams is to be able to manipulate and control certain kinds of information that seem to be available to us in a random, nonlogical, or subtle way. This desire can be seen in our frustration as we struggle at times to convey the sensation of a dream. Try as we might, some of the fundamental conclusions contained in that reflection without a subject, without a clearly defined ego, gain a much hazier form in the world of speech and of concepts than what we felt in our dream. As we analyzed above, this lack of clarity derives from our desire to isolate the specificities of what was dreamed without reconstituting the background, the medium in which these specificities were fixed within the reality of the dream.

Once in a while, however, intuition expresses itself quite specifically within the apparent world. On these occasions we may have a presentiment of something that allows us to make use of this knowledge leaked from the hidden world as if it were an element of the realm of the apparent. Premonitions occur when something seems to break free from the objective logic of cause and effect, to gain form. This rupture is felt because what identifies a specific form is not other forms but a medium from which the intuitor has retrieved this form.

If we are to try intervening in the hidden realm of our own volition, we must better define relations between the apparent and the hidden.

Rabbi Naftali of Ropshitz received the Rabbi of Kozwitz as his guest. When he entered the house, the guest stared in thought at a window with its curtains closed. When the host commented on this apparent curiosity, the Rabbi of Kozwitz explained what interested him so much: "If you want people to peer inside, why have curtains? And if you don't want them to, why have a window?"

Rabbi Naftali replied, "Because when I want someone I love very much to look inside, I open the curtains."

This is an important exchange, one that employs intriguing images. The window and the curtain permit a relationship that is both veiled and revealed. A home is a defined space, the dwelling place of consciousness. The "outside" is a vast unknown; it is the whole that contains countless forms we cannot distinguish. The suggestion that there is a contradiction between having a window and concealing it with curtains reflects the fact that the very instrument of unveiling is also an instrument of veiling. When the biblical text speaks of the bitterness of eyes that do not see and ears that do not hear, this is a reference to windows whose curtains are closed. The faculties of the apparent world are themselves barriers to the hidden world: the harder you try to see, the more you will fail; the harder you try to hear, the more you will fail. Your intervention will not work by controlling what is apparent, for this makes it impossible to access what is hidden.

Rabbi Naftali's response—"When I want someone I love very much to look inside, I open the curtains"—presumes some form of intervention. What does "someone I love very much" mean? It perhaps refers to an intense desire that is not rational, that involves forms of perception subtler than the senses. The biblical verses in which God most eloquently addresses humans (Deuteronomy 6:4–6), in which the hidden (the essence) is directed toward revealing the apparent (the form), tell us:

Hear, O Israel [differentiated world]: the Lord [your essence]—Yah—is our God, the Lord [your medium] is one [undifferentiated]. You shall love the Lord your God [your essence] with all your heart and with all your soul and with all your strength. These commandments that I give you today are to be upon your hearts.

Loving the essence is what leaves us windows so we won't miss a possible link into something we cannot apprehend save through this instrument we call "love." But why do we have to be able to open the curtains? So that what is conveyed by the realm of the hidden may be upon our hearts. It is not via our senses that what comes in through the window gains form. This can only happen when something circles our heart, is upon our heart—until, for some reason unknown to us, this knowledge penetrates the heart. The opening of the curtain or armor of the heart (the instrument of love) lends apparent form to something that was hidden—something that the tools of reason would not perceive.

How can we intervene in the intuitive universe? By not intervening, by allowing the answers to first appear and only then to retrieve the question. If you accept these intuitive answers and let them circle your heart, it is possible that the precise question will eventually retrieve one of these circling answers. At that moment something whose source will be a mystery to other people will gain form within the realm of the apparent. Others will ask themselves: "What was the question that made this answer possible?" And they will never discover. They will not know that the process which wrought this form was not the act of answering but the act of retrieving the question.

This is why intervening in the intuitive universe entails letting go more than controlling. Let us examine this Hasidic tale:

A man who lived in the same city as Rabbi Sussia was filled with emotion when he saw the state of poverty in which this devout sage lived. So every day he would leave a sum of money in the purse where the Rebbe kept his *tefillin* (phylacteries). With this money, Rabbi Sussia could at least feed his children. From the day the man began to practice this act of charity, he grew wealthier and wealthier. And the wealthier he grew, the more he gave to Rabbi Sussia, and even more wealth would he then accrue.

One day, however, the man suddenly realized that Rabbi Sussia was a disciple of a great Maggid, and it struck him that if his charity toward a disciple was so lavishly rewarded, maybe he would become even wealthier if he contributed directly to the master. And so he did. He traveled to the master's city and talked him into accepting a donation.

From that moment on, the man's assets began to dwindle, until he eventually lost everything he had amassed during his period of prosperity. Ridden with anxiety, the man consulted with Rabbi Sussia and told him the whole story, explaining that he'd taken this action because the Rebbe himself told him that his master was much more powerful.

Rabbi Sussia replied, "Look: as long as you were contributing and were not concerned about whom you were giving to—be it Rabbi Sussia or someone else—God gave to you without concerning Himself about whom He was giving to. But when you began to search out people who were particularly notable recipients, God did the exact same thing."

This story shows us that the moment this man established a relationship of control, of reasoning—"this is more important than that"—he interrupted a process of a different nature. Just as our organisms are possessed of "parasympathetic" systems— like the one that keeps us breathing—over which we have no conscious control, there is a similar modality within thought: a vegetative perception of reasoning—literally, of a "vegetable" order that differs from our "animal" reasoning, which seeks to subjugate and dominate a piece of information in order to comprehend it. The world of vegetation exists more as a medium than as differentiated form, in contrast with the animal world. The medium—the forests, the realm that the plant world inhabits—is much less readily distinguishable than the medium of the animal kingdom. Like the sea, the forest is a medium filled with forms, but there is a much smaller difference in "density" between medium and species (form) than there is in the case of animals.

Therefore the animal dimension is a greater approximation of the rational world, whereas the plant dimension represents the intuitive world.

What might seem to be a minor detail is well worth looking at: a linguistic distinction we make without thinking. When we want to bring others "to their senses," summon them to the territory of logic, we use the verb *look*. "Look here" is a call for us to be logical and sensible. But when God says, "O Israel (form), listen!" He is summoning us to the hidden world. That is why in colloquial language we say we should "listen to our heart." We don't say we should let our heart "look," nor do we refer to having listened to our consciousness. Within the realm of the hidden, of the dissimulated, there lies something that we gain access to by "listening," something that our faculty of sight fails to capture.

What is essential is that we know there are ways of intervening in, lending legitimacy to, and even fostering our intuitive processes. But these processes cannot be submitted to any of the modalities of manipulation feasible within the apparent dimension. The tale above—as a fine illustration of this—teaches us a valuable lesson. In applying an act of purposeful selection and logic to his relation with the hidden, the man ends up entering this very realm of hiddenness. From a revealing force, logic becomes an effacing one. The desire to apply the condition of logic to a hidden reality ("If donating to this man has this result, donating to a more powerful man should intensify this result") becomes the very barrier to the interaction that had been taking place. In other words, the person wanted to introduce "form" into that relation and simply ended up confined to the dimension of "forms." What he had been perceiving as "medium" ("He is poor; I must help"), he endeavored to make fit within a perception of form, and he found himself solely and exclusively faced with "forms," thus losing his link to the hidden world.

How Absurdity Helps to Reveal the Hidden

In his stories, the Yiddish writer Sholom Aleichem created a village called Chelm that became legendary in Jewish folklore. An unfortunate accident took place in this village. The stork that distributes souls around the world always deposits a certain number of wise souls and a certain number of foolish souls within each region of the planet. But in the case of Chelm, the stork mistakenly spilled out a sack filled with nothing but foolish souls. The village had no choice but to select its leaders from among these souls—including its wise rabbis. Ever since, Chelm has been famed as a land of folly. Yet this laboratory of the illogical has likewise become the source of great teachings the world over.

Let us get acquainted with Chelm. The village rabbi will act as our guide. We'll begin by listening to some of the questions the citizens of Chelm have brought their sage—and to his vital answers:

A man from Chelm asked, "Why is the ocean salty?"

The rabbi confidently replied, "Elementary! Because it's full of herring."

"And why does a man's hair go gray before his beard?"

"Obvious! After all, the hair is at least thirteen years older than the beard," the rabbi replied, scratching the hair on his own chin.

"And why does a dog wag his tail?"

"This one," the rabbi said with a grin, "is even easier. It's obvious a dog wags its tail because the tail is lighter than the dog. Were the tail heavier, the tail would wag the dog!"

Here is another example of sophisticated Chelm logic:

Two men from Chelm went for a walk. One took his umbrella and the other didn't. In the middle of their stroll it began to rain.

"Open your umbrella," suggested the man who hadn't brought his.

"It won't do any good," the other responded.

"What do you mean, it won't do any good? It will keep the rain off us!"

"But the umbrella is so full of holes it looks like a strainer."

"So why did you bring it?" the first one asked in perplexity.

"I didn't think it was going to rain!"

We can tell that Chelm is a place we could easily not take seriously, and were it not merely a figment of Yiddish folklore's imagination, it would be crawling with researchers. Scholars of semiotics, logic, psychoanalysis, and even parapsychology would be investigating the hidden world that fools can unveil for us. This is because fools live in a world where the medium is high in density, like water. It is a world of forms that readily and constantly blend into their surroundings. Let us examine some examples of how the fools inhabiting this obscure little town are often the emissaries of hard-to-reach knowledge.

Questions sourced from the hidden sphere can be classified as displaying one of these three characteristics: (1) reversibility, (2) forms that fade away as they blend with a medium more apparent than the forms themselves, and (3) a tendency for the internal and external to merge.

Reversibility can be detected in all the examples from Chelm mentioned earlier. Notice that as each question is presented, the rabbi redefines a new question that is in fact a derivative of the answer to the original question. It is herring that makes the sea salty—as human perception takes precedence in defining cause and effect. Anyone observing from the apparent world can't help poking fun at the fool. But as we shall see later on, the trouble is that the fool can achieve an efficacity that leaves a rationalist dumbfounded. Perpetually retrieving a question that is existential in nature, curiosity for the sake of curiosity remains unanswered.

When the question comes cloaked in a guise of existentialism, it will be turned inside out, transfigured into an answer that begs another question of a logical nature. The question "Why does a dog wag its tail?" elicits the kind of reply expected if it were an inquiry from the field of physics, of the study of inertia. There is no way to fool a fool. However much we disguise our questions born of curiosity, the fool will always strip them bare by transforming them into absurdities—and these absurdities reveal hidden existential perspectives. What matters here is that when the fool gets the question backwards and therefore changes it, he moves toward an answer that could not be as thoroughly understood were it not for its absurdist aspect. In short, absurdity reveals more about the hidden realm of things than any type of rationalism can.

In the second case—where the medium is more apparent than the form itself—absurdity also plays a fundamental role.

Two men from Chelm were debating which is more important, the sun or the moon.

One held that the sun is more important because it is bigger and brighter than the moon.

The other insisted, "You're wrong! The moon is more important than the sun. Without the light of the moon, our nights would be so dark nobody could see an inch in front of their nose. But the sun shines by day—when it's light out anyway!"

Here logic merges with the medium: light. The question itself dissolves because an absurdist answer exposes the existential importance of an astral body. The moon is "obviously" more important to human beings since it is benevolent precisely when humans are more afraid—at night. From this viewpoint, sunlight does little good; "it only shines during the day," when we are less afraid. The medium—that is, fear; that is, what we humans deem of greater relevance—stands out in contrast with our logical expectations. In other words, when analyzed more carefully, an anecdote we might simply dismiss as "absurd" has much to teach us about human processes.

The third case—the melding of interiors and exteriors—is illustrated by this tale of a small house in Chelm. Ethel and her husband, Sam, are in bed.

A window had been left ajar, and Ethel was freezing as a draft of frigid winter wind swept through the crack. Sam lay next to her snoring away, oblivious to his wife's discomfort.

It got to the point where Ethel couldn't stand it anymore. Shaking her husband, she complained, "Sam, Sam, it's cold outside! Go shut the window!"

Sam didn't budge. Ethel persisted, shaking her husband even harder. "Get up and close the window. It's really cold out there!"

Now Sam was wide awake—and furious. "And you think if I close the window it'll get any warmer outside?"

Absurdity has once again retrieved the real issue: "Good grief! You can't get a good night's sleep in this house!" Well outside the bounds of logic, Sam's answer has uncamouflaged the hidden realm of Ethel's text, "It's cold outside." Sam's solution to what is apparently the problem is the way Sam finds to question his wife's good sense. This good sense has nothing to do with whether it's cold or warm but whether or not Sam has been woken up at an acceptable hour.

Absurdity can yield knowledge and help account for reality only when we are able to focus on the medium instead of on any specific forms it produces.

Absurdity is unique in its capacity to elucidate certain states of consciousness. Here is another telling tale from Chelm:

> A man from Chelm decided to leave his family and move to the big city. His curiosity about city life got the better of him, and he managed to summon up the courage to leave. On his first night away from home, he put up at a boardinghouse. Before going to bed, he placed his shoes on the floor pointing in the direction he should head the next day. During the night, the fellow who ran the boardinghouse decided to play a trick on the villager, turning his shoes around and pointing them in the opposite direction—the direction from which he had come.
>
> When the man from Chelm awoke the next day, he looked at the direction in which his shoes were pointing, put them on, and headed out for the "big city." Much to his surprise, it wasn't as big as he thought. In point of fact, it looked a lot like his hometown. What was really amazing was that there in the big city he stumbled across a street much like his, a house much like his, and even a family just like the one he had left behind. He adapted so well that he ended up spending the rest of his life in the big city.

The villager's ability to not wake up, to sustain his journey at all costs, was what allowed him to find his real place in life. The big city is here and now. The logic of destiny decided by turned-around shoes, the logic of painting a target after shooting your arrow, can teach us much about the possibilities life affords us. His dream realized, the fellow from Chelm found the big city in a much broader, deeper sense, and life gave him a sweet destiny. All thanks to his ability to deal with hiddenness, to understand the medium of which form—in this case, his trip—was a part.

The Efficiency of the Fool

Within the Apparent Realm of What Is Hidden, half a sage is useless. This inefficacy in the face of hiddenness is so glaring that he or she is often the butt of great sarcasm. The German author Berthold Auerbach made this observation: "There are some clever people who may be compared to the small fashionable shops: all the merchandise is displayed in the show window."[10] They can only relate to what is within the territory of concrete logic. And the nineteenth-century humorist Moritz Saphir pointed out, "Clever people are like fragrant roses; when you smell one rose it's delightful, but smelling a whole bouquet you may get quite a headache."[11] In this terrain only complete sages or complete fools survive. Since there are few enough of the former and an abundance of the latter, the fool's role in uncovering hidden secrets has acquired mythic status.

Here's an enlightening anecdote:

As legend goes, during the Middle Ages the pope decided the Jews should no longer live in Rome; they should all be banished. The Jews grew afraid, for outside of Rome lay the darkness of rural medieval Europe. They begged to be allowed to stay.

The pope listened to their pleas and agreed to give them just one chance. But he set forth a very strange condition. He would permit a debate—all in pantomime—pitting a nuncio against any Jew. If the Jew should win, his people could stay in Rome. Otherwise, out they would go.

But what kind of possibility was this, the Jews wondered. The pope himself was to be the judge of the debate and the losing debater would be executed. How could anyone win against such a set-up! No one in the Jewish community could possibly accept the role.

But the sweeper of the synagogue volunteered. He would debate. Everyone knew the sweeper was surely going to his death. But what could they do! There was no way to save him

---

10. Ausubel.
11. Ibid.

from death and the Jewish community from exile. There was
not even any way that the Jewish scholars could prepare the
sweeper for the debate.

The day of the debate came. Everybody sat in the arena
in complete silence.

The nuncio began by raising one finger and moving it
across the sky. The sweeper instantly gestured firmly at the
ground. The pope looked uneasy.

Then the nuncio lifted one finger again, and this time
pointed it squarely at the sweeper's face. The sweeper
quickly pointed three fingers at the nuncio with complete as-
surance. And now the pope really looked uncomfortable.

The nuncio now reached deep into his pocket and withdrew an apple, which he showed to the pope. At this, the
sweeper took out a paper bag from his pocket, and withdrew
a piece of matzoh.

The pope now announced that the debate was over. The
sweeper had won; the Jews could stay in Rome.

"Your Holiness!" cried the churchmen when the crowd
had dispersed, "Why did you award the Jew the verdict?"

"That man," answered the pope, "was a master of debate.
When my nuncio swept his hand across the heavens to indicate that God ruled over everything, the Jew gestured toward
the ground, indicating that the Devil also held sway of a world
all his own!

"When my nuncio lifted one finger to indicate that there
was only one God, the Jew instantly lifted three fingers to
indicate the three aspects of God, the Holy Trinity.

"When my nuncio took out an apple to indicate the error
of science that teaches the earth is round as an apple, the
Jew countered by producing a flat piece of matzoh, to show
that the Bible teaches the earth is flat."

The Jews, overjoyed, toasted and feasted their beadle.
Then they begged him to explain how he had bested the
nuncio.

"What's there to say?" he answered. "First, the priest

waved his hand like he's saying 'The Jews must get out of Rome.' So I pointed downward to say 'Oh yeah! The Jews are going to stay right here!'

"Next, he points a finger at me as if to say 'Drop dead! The Jews are leaving.' So I point three fingers at him to say, 'You drop dead three times. The Jews are staying.' "

"And then?" asked the amazed congregation.

"And then I saw he was taking out his lunch, so I took out mine!"[12]

In his own nonsensical fashion the fool achieved the impossible. By reducing it to the vacuity of partial sapience, of half-wisdom, he showed how the notion of *impossible* is in fact unsound. No sage could envisage having the slightest chances of winning the debate. But it certainly could be won—it was merely necessary for someone to look at it from another angle, from another plane of reality, armed with the firm conviction that "the Jews must stay." The fool's indignation, which drives the debate, places him not on the plane of threats but instead shows he does not cower before the burden of wisdom. His logic is pathetic yet efficacious. Although totally wrong, his reading of reality is mighty when it comes to intervening in this reality. The fool knows without knowing. Better put: the fool distinguishes the medium and confronts the desire for form, for answers, armed solely with his awareness of the medium. The half-wise, who distinguish and cling to forms, are caught in surprise by the legitimacy of that which is undifferentiated.

In short, paying heed to the fool's reading of reality can produce results not to be found within the world of the apparent. The fool draws his reasons from the hidden world, and when he unveils them, the half-sage sees answers within the apparent world. The fool is an instrument; our foolishness and naiveté

---

12. Simon R. Pollack, *Jewish Wit for All Occasions* (New York: A&W, 1979), pp. 176–79.

are instruments that allow us to break through barriers to the impossible. As the Yiddish saying goes: "When a task is overwhelming, when you've got too much to do, go to sleep!" *Gey shlofen* (Yiddish for "Go to sleep") is a kind of artifice that lets us draw on energies less tainted by weary, worn-out ways of thinking. By bringing forth our naive side, this artifice affords us the possibility of understanding mediums and environments—and from this vantage point it becomes possible to "undisguise" the vicious circles where our thoughts and decision-making processes are easily imprisoned as they grope toward "cleverness" and "sagacity."

Achieving the Impossible

I would like to use a true story to illustrate how decisions can be based on an understanding and mastery of realities found within the apparent realm of the hidden world.

In a certain town, on the eve of a wedding, a terrible groaning can be heard coming from the backyard of the bride's house. Everyone is frightened by the spine-chilling howl. After all, Jewish tradition says brides are dangerously vulnerable on the night before their weddings. This is why it is customary for a vigil to take place on the eve of the ceremony to ward off any evil spirits or such—particularly evil thoughts—that might take unfair advantage of this vulnerability. It was this folklore that inspired Solomon Ansky's famous play, *The Dybbuk*, which narrates the tale of a bride possessed by an evil spirit. The belief may stem from the fact that until not so very long ago, brides were just young girls, and it was traumatic for them to leave their parents' home to start life with a man they often met only on their wedding day. It was not unusual for this to trigger nervous crises or fits.

In any case, terrifying cries from the backyard on the eve of a young woman's wedding day was a matter for concern. The local rabbi was quickly taken to the scene to ascertain just what was happening. Arriving there, he heard the bloodcurdling howls coming from the backyard and was himself quite frightened. He decided it would be too dangerous to investigate personally, and so he called for the town fool—the local madman—who could be sent to see what was wrong. The rabbi was convinced that what was happening was not merely dangerous but also of great complexity.

The fool was brought to the house and sent off toward the terrifying sound. A little while later he came back looking quite at ease. Everyone rushed over to find out what was going on. The fool calmly explained that there was no cause for worry. According to him, the screams were easily accounted for. An old tree had toppled over, and its trunk was lying across the ground. As time went by the trunk had hollowed out, and the wind whipping through it now produced this terrible noise. But it was nothing more than a kind of eerie sound effect caused by wind blowing through a rotting tree.

Everyone but the rabbi was relieved. That night he gathered the community together and recommended that they pack their suitcases: they must leave. For the rabbi, the sign was self-evident. Nobody understood, but all nevertheless followed his recommendation.

This rabbi was the leader of a small village in Poland, and his entire community was saved from the Nazi insanity that would reign shortly thereafter.

The rabbi heard cries that were very real: cries that came from the future, cries that would overwhelmingly challenge the imagination of anyone who ventured to foresee these horrors. So the wailing was quite real. But how could the rabbi decipher all this from the information at hand?

Let us try to reconstruct the events. A howling sound from the house of a bride on the eve of her wedding—here is our first piece of information. The fool is brought in, and he hands over a rational, convincing interpretation of an explainable natural phenomenon. The rabbi is skeptical. After all, he had called in the fool because the fool would be more open to any hidden reality that he might encounter. Rather than returning from the backyard with an absurd tale to tell, one blending fantasy and superstition, the fool comes back with a discourse that is not a fool's discourse at all. It is a discourse that enlightens on the plane of the Apparent Realm of What Is Apparent. But fools do not see the Apparent Realm of What Is Apparent—that is why they are fools or mad people. Ergo the rabbi's conclusion: what seems to be the Apparent Realm of What Is Apparent is not. It was only presented in this form because the fool had made contact with that which is hidden. It was the hidden realm that afforded him this sense of the Apparent Realm of What Is Apparent—something that would not be perceived by someone else. We now realize that when the rabbi summoned the madman he was not cruelly throwing a fool in to take his chances where a wise man feared to tread. The fool was an instrument: by using his naiveté, the rabbi measured the presence of hidden elements.

The rabbi's order for all to flee—complied with unquestioningly—reflects the wise person's effective ability to use hidden information to intervene in apparent reality. Everyone respected the allusive elements, and this way of seeing things saved them. The rabbi respected the qualities inherent in a fool and recognized his legitimacy, while the community respected the qualities inherent in a sage and in turn recognized his legitimacy. By turning values inside out—a madman speaks wisely while a rabbi speaks superstitiously—the villagers retrieved information not available within the realm of appearances.

There is actually a sort of formula for accessing this type of knowledge. It is essential to know how to use the tools that can penetrate this dimension of the Apparent Realm of What Is Hidden in order to then invert values or apply absurd logic. These instruments are represented by the fool inside each one of us:

our naivetés, feelings, premonitions, dreams, recurring images, mysteries from the past, the coincidences that befall us. There are ways we can understand this information and put it to good use. A word of caution is of course necessary: if no element of wisdom is applied in deciphering any information retrieved from the hidden realm into the Apparent Realm of What Is Apparent, we may end up simply acting like fools. A fool has the information but doesn't know how to use it.

It therefore requires judiciousness and humility on our part to make sense of the information constantly circling around and appearing before us. Our problem is that the fool inside is often times not awake, and our half-sage disqualifies information as absurd and useless. Or perhaps the problem lies not in whether we employ the fool within us correctly but in how poorly we use our inner sage as a partner in deciphering that which we manage to apprehend.

Be this as it may, the Apparent Realm of What Is Hidden is of utmost importance. The survivors of this small village bear witness. It conforms to the reality of the hidden but can still be made apparent, or manifest. Because there are still fragments of discernment contained within this realm, it may ultimately give rise to concrete plans of action and intervention, as seen in the events described above.

In everything we have examined so far, the apparent dimension has somehow been present—as the Apparent Realm of What Is Apparent, or the Hidden Realm of What Is Apparent, or the Apparent Realm of What Is Hidden. We are about to enter a new dimension, where there is no more a priori discernment, a territory where no courses of action will emerge from our discernment—a realm even more hidden.

REVERENCE

THE HIDDEN REALM OF WHAT IS HIDDEN

The designs in a person's mind are deep waters,
but a person of understanding can draw them out.

—Proverbs 20:5

In the Hidden Realm of What Is Hidden, Pascal's celebrated phrase has great bearing: "The heart has its reasons that reason knows nothing of." There is no room here for strategies of reason because this territory is bereft of any vestige of visible elements. All is hidden, all lies beyond knowledge. We might then ask why we should even include this dimension within the "orchard." Isn't this orchard the total sum of all possible space for human instruction and learning?

The Hidden Realm of What Is Hidden is still a realm that can be revealed, and thus it is accessible to human beings. However, it can be accessed only through action, not through reason.

In addressing this issue, Martin Buber distinguishes two important areas of human experience: discernment and commitment. Action is a commitment, a means of intervention triggered by our discernment at a certain point in time. According to Buber, whenever an individual discerns something, a level of

commitment will occur as the outcome—and vice versa: a commitment engenders discernment. When we come to understand
something at its deepest level, that is, when we internalize something, it will impact our behavior and the way we think. This is
what the realm of the apparent reveals. We are able to intervene
in our way of being and thinking when we understand previously
hidden aspects and manifest these through concrete action.

The revolutionary aspect of this thought lies within the corol-
lary that states that any form of action can also foster discernment. What this means is that when we act, we penetrate the
hidden dimension and set discernment free at the level of the
apparent world.

In this story attributed to Reb Zalman Schachter-Shalomi, a
disciple inquires about wisdom:

> "How can one achieve wisdom, sagacity, and under-
> standing?"
> "Through good sense and good judgment."
> "And how can one achieve 'good judgment'?"
> "Through much experience."
> "And how can one acquire much experience?"
> "Through bad judgments!"

Experience, action, and ensuing error afford us an opportunity to inject information into reason's arid territories. This use
of deeds—that is, of commitment—to fertilize and elucidate our
discernment represents the Hidden Realm of What Is Hidden.

One of Jewish tradition's greatest legacies to Western civilization is precisely this inverted perception, which has never been
well understood or applied very much to problem solving. It is
an insight that first occurred when the Israelites discovered the
secret of making "the waters part." According to Jewish interpretive tradition, it was thanks to what we read in Exodus 24:7 that
the sea could be divided. In this verse, Israel lets Moses know

that it will obey divine purposes: "All that the Lord has said will we do and then hear." This intentional inversion of *do* and *hear*—commitment and discernment—is the paradigmatic revolutionary element to which I am referring. The Hebrews' perception, which contrasted sharply with conventional modes of conduct, was a product of their experience of being cornered.

According to tradition, before the sea could open, a man by the name of Nachshon, who didn't know how to swim, had to jump in. It was his deed that allowed the Israelites to understand that the seas could be divided. From that point on, no matter how fleeting the nature of this perception, human consciousness has been eternally aware that cognition depends upon *being* as an alternative to reasoning and imagining. The Rabbi of Kotzk put it succinctly:

> There are so many wise academics and philosophers in the world, all investigating, pondering, and delving into God's mysteries. . . . And why do they get lost in their wisdom? This happens because they are trapped and held back by their intellectual faculties and perceptive abilities. The people of Israel, however, received a powerful tool for raising their perceptive ability beyond the intellect to reach the level of heavenly angels. And what tool was this? God's commandments (*mitzvot*).

The sacralization of commitments was a way of affirming that cognition also takes place at another level, beyond the level of the intellect and of sensory perception. *Pirkei Avot* (4:6) puts this in terms of a kind of formula: "He who learns in order to teach is granted the means to learn and to teach; but he who learns in order to practice is granted the means to learn and to teach, to observe and to practice." Whoever delves into the hidden realm of understanding will not only obtain access to the apparent realm but will become master of that which is not apparent.

The secret of this hidden region of cognition once again lies within the realm of "the answer that finds its question." This reversibility undoes the conventional belief that *action* follows *decision*. Here, action can perfectly well influence any decision made. This is the great contribution of "We will do and then hear"—there are no favored hierarchies within the world of knowledge. Certain commitments teach us what no form of deduction ever can.

Mistakes: The First Step toward Success

When we looked at the hidden realm and its characteristics, we saw how it can bring forth answers to dynamic questions that are in a state of constant mutation, unlike the apparent level, which deals solely with static situations. An example from science itself serves as a good illustration of this "dynamic" style of answer.

The scientific community was quite excited to discover the mechanism of DNA repair. DNA is a complex molecule that encodes all the information that manifests itself in physical form as a unique individual. Any alteration in these singular codes will immediately be reflected in the physical organism.

Scientists were surprised to discover that DNA operates by allowing a large number of errors to occur during replication. After all, this production of errors does not seem typical of nature's way of doing things, with its tendency to favor extremely efficacious and efficient evolution. So how can this fundamental structure be considered efficient if it is steadily producing errors?

The cell biologist Miriam Stampfer explains:

> In designing a coding material, the solution that turns out to be most efficient overall (given the natural limitations present in the building blocks of the physical world) is not to employ

material that is always constant, stable, error free. Rather, it is to allow a fair degree of errors (as occurs with the DNA coding material) and design in parallel very efficient error recognition and repair mechanisms.[13]

In other words, DNA has found the "perfect" way of dealing with the limitations of the physical world, employing a sophisticated system of defects whose repair will lead to a refined way of getting it right.

In like fashion, we humans can learn from what is concealed or inconspicuous, using a method that depends upon errors. As Reb Zalman said, "Learn your good judgments from your bad ones." DNA *does* first, then *hears* and *judges*.

Making it a habit to admit your own foolishness and mistakes is often a much better way of learning than attaining knowledge through books and theoretical concepts. "He whose deeds exceed his wisdom, his wisdom endures; but he whose wisdom exceeds his deeds, his wisdom does not endure," according to *Pirkei Avot* (3:12). DNA wants to endure, so it sets about *doing* more than *discerning*.

No progress can be made in problem solving unless some empirical measure underpins that which is thought. Recognizing these limits of discernment is an important first step. Knowing how to retrieve something edible from this part of the orchard is a truly difficult task. In this world, getting it right is a disaster: it merely confirms what can already be confirmed. This world, where someone who gets it right misses the chance to know the incredible world of "isn't," is a kind of literality of hiddenness.

As we saw earlier, it is the literalist's job (in the Apparent Realm of What Is Apparent) to identify what was not said within that which was said, and with this information in hand to better understand the question. Within the Hidden Realm of What Is

---

13. *New Menorah*, Summer 1994.

Hidden, what matters is recognizing your mistake—the unspoken part of an action—so that you can better understand and identify what you got right. The wholly apparent and the wholly hidden thus meet. The mistake surrounding the action is to the cognition of hiddenness as the ignorance surrounding information is to our understanding of the apparent.

The Hazards of Not Making Mistakes

Mistakes are fundamental to deriving cognition from the hidden realm. If you don't make enough mistakes, you have no way of using the knowledge and discernment they engender. How can we ascertain that we are not making progress in solving a problem or dealing with an issue because we have not made enough mistakes?

Of course, mistakes are not something we should strive to make. If we tried to follow Nachshon's lead and throw ourselves into the Red Sea without knowing how to swim, the waters would not part for us. We would be making an irreversible mistake, because in this case there is no doubt about the Apparent Realm of What Is Apparent: if you don't know how to swim, you shouldn't jump into the ocean. This is the error committed by the person who "dies" upon venturing into the orchard, referring back to the symbology of the sages. He "dies" because he doesn't know how to swim. In dealing with a given problem, this is tantamount to following a path to resolution that discards the rational process. True mistakes—those whose teachings derive from the hidden realm—do not come about because we have discarded rational processes. They are the products of real experience, where we have more than exhausted our ability to discern. It is only when we have laid claim to all possible alternatives and conclusions made available by our discernment that the act of throwing oneself into the sea does not have the outcome that befell the Egyptians.

Depression, for example, is a human reaction triggered when we do not have enough experiences that produce mistakes, which allow us to move forward. The feeling that we are failing to make full use of our life experiences leaves us with the painful sensation that we are "being left behind," that we are missing out on valuable knowledge. This hidden knowledge is essential to validating the world of our discernment, making sense out of that which cannot be perceived in any other way. Making sense of and resolving what has yet to be explained is only possible through the dimension of action, of hiddenness.

> The Rabbi of Kotzk asks: "What is the meaning of the commandment 'Do not steal'?"
>
> His disciples reply, "That's obvious: it means 'Do not rob your neighbor.' "
>
> "No," responds the Rabbi. "It means 'Do not rob yourself.' "

What is "not robbing yourself"? Leaving yourself wide open. If you do not leave yourself wide open to life, if you protect yourself from life, you are robbing yourself of fundamental instructions about yourself and about life that cannot be obtained through discernment. No one can convey the knowledge acquired through another person's experience, because this knowledge is not merely a piece of information but rather a sophisticated referential that exposes all mistakes (or ignorances) having to do with being in that particular position. When you try to teach what you have learned from experience but without understanding that the nature of this knowledge is hidden from someone who hasn't experienced it, it is like pointing to a place on a map when there's no map there. It does no good to point because the reference points are missing.

The Rabbi of Kobrin once said, "If it were within my power, I would hide all the teachings of the sages, for when someone has much knowledge, there is a risk that this knowledge will greatly exceed his acts."

The Rabbi of Kobrin is expressing his concern over the vast difference between those who have vessels to hold information and those who lack experience. This difference becomes more striking when apparent knowledge stripped of its hidden dimension is compared with teachings that include information acquired by the experience and exposure inherent to the hidden realm. An example is found in the Hasidic tale of a disciple who seeks out a master with whom to study; only a few days later, the disciple is authorized by the master to be a master himself. The other disciples question this decision: "How could he have received so much knowledge in such a short time?" The master explains: "He is a person who came to me with many candles. All I did was light a single one: by himself he was able to light all the others, as well as his own path."

Knowledge of the hidden realm is represented by these candles ready to be lit within the apparent realm. Their potential as vessels of light is important not only because they illuminate but above all because they legitimate and render perceivable all other areas where candles are ready to be lit. These candles are made of the wax of our mistakes and bad judgments. When this wax is in short supply, we are "made stupid." The prime symptom that wax is lacking is that the individual fails to recognize all the candles ready to be lit. The creativity dwelling at these depths—where the medium absorbs forms—is derived from the act of perceiving all that is ready to be lit within the hidden realm and to thus ignite discernment.

Educational Metamodels

One of the great challenges in education is to keep discernment and commitment in adequate proportions. When students become dull, it is often because their education favors discernment over experience; it places great value on light but does not teach how to recognize nearby candles that have the potential to shed light as well. Reb Bunam addresses the problem in these terms: "On the Sabbath, when my classroom is full, I find it very hard to teach Torah, because each and every person needs his own understanding of Torah, and each one seeks his own perfection. So what I give to all, I take away from all."

When something is reduced to pure discernment, any teaching subtracts instead of adding. Generalizations, which might be defined as everything that has been lived and experienced by more than one individual, tend to create roadblocks to the hidden world of action. Generalizations omit or exaggerate details and cause teaching to hamper true understanding. How can you talk to everyone? By talking about what is apparent. And when you talk about what is apparent, what is obscured? That which is hidden. "When a student exclaims, 'Aha! I got it!' a good teacher's heart sinks; for the good teacher realizes that the student's grasp of a general principle means a loss of real learning that springs from individual experience."

Another style of teaching needs to be combined with education that is designed for everyone—but that costs everyone so much. Reb Mendel explains it this way:

> I became a Hasid because there was an old man in the town where I lived who told stories about the saintly people of the past. He told me everything he knew, and I understood what I needed to.

When a teacher shares his or her knowledge and each student knows how to retrieve from the whole the part that he or she needs, then this information migrates to the territory of experience. This kind of teaching urges disciples to investigate their possible "candles." The teacher's flame does not light a single, particular candle but is offered to the students so that they may kindle whatever they need to. Such a teacher recognizes that the hidden world manufactures candles, and that just as fire can light them, so can it outshine them.

It is essential for everyone to have his or her own way of retaining and maintaining light. When a young disciple complained that he was losing his zeal in the search for knowledge and questioning, the Rabbi of Rizin replied, "You are like someone walking with a guide through the forest on a dark night. As soon as the guide moves away from you, darkness takes over. But if you carry your own light, you need not fear the darkness."

Only a teacher who has studied with this purpose in mind can make it possible for his students to light their own candles. As Reb Bunam puts it, "A bad teacher says what he knows; a good teacher knows what he says." The teacher's involvement and his hidden side play a role in the conception of thoughts and in the process of distinguishing. He guides his disciples toward internalization and awakens their commitments on the road to discernment. Rabbi Yitzchak of Vorki tells how this can be accomplished:

> A merchant who wanted to go on a trip hired a clerk to work in his shop, with the hope that he could trust the clerk to run the business in his absence. To make sure, the merchant decided to work in a room next to the shop so that he could hear everything going on there. During the first year he would sometimes hear his clerk tell a customer, "The boss won't let me give you that kind of discount." And so the merchant didn't take his trip. The second year he would sometimes hear, "We can't give you that kind of discount." And again the merchant wouldn't take his trip. The third year he began hearing, "I can't give you that kind of discount." That's when he set out on his trip.

A good teacher can leave only when he knows the disciples can discern from their own experience. Unless knowledge enjoys access to the Hidden Realm of What Is Hidden, it cannot be maintained; it fades away into the meaninglessness to which everything is subject when this hidden component is lacking. This is why the teachings of a true master cannot be conveyed by reason.

The Rabbi of Kalev was once urged to reveal what his master had taught him. He replied, "My master's teachings are like manna that enters the body and never leaves it." Pushed harder to reveal his secrets, the rabbi ripped open his shirt and exclaimed, "Look inside my heart! There you will understand where my master's teachings lie."

The teachings do not lie within the realm of reason but have been planted in the heart, in the realms of feeling and of experience. Teachings that include the Hidden Realm of What Is Hidden are experienced much more than understood. That is why the following comment appears in the Jerusalem Talmud: "I learned much from my masters, and even more from my peers than from my teachers, and even more from my students than from my peers." Whoever teaches as a modality of experience will of course learn as well from what is taught. And whoever learns with the purpose of doing will also do and also discern. Bernard Shaw's words may be fitting here: "He who can does. He who cannot teaches."

Unknown Knowledge

The Baal Shem Tov once said, "When I reach the highest levels of knowledge, I know that not a single letter of the teachings is in me." The hidden realm encompasses all of this unmastered domain. Hiddenness knows that memory is an instance of form and that there is no dense medium within the memory: everything is recorded according to specific details or characteristics. The hidden realm does not deal with objective memory but stores its data in atmospheres and environments. These environments may be physical (smells, visual images), emotional (a special occasion, a certain setting), or existential (being trapped, embarking on a new love).

A person who dwells in environments is someone in motion, someone who experiences life and remains open to it at any given moment. On the other hand, objectivity, or the detached eye of apparent knowledge, manages to constrain things into form and memorize them.

The big problem is communication between these two worlds. Some people may argue, "But isn't the apparent realm a representation of that which is apparent? How can this other, hidden knowledge be grasped without perverting what is apparent?" And others will ask, "How can we understand the hidden realm without making it apparent? Yet how *could* it become apparent, as that would detract from its very nature?"

It is vital to recognize that the hidden realm possesses a kind of knowledge that is not knowledge, which at no point seeks to render itself apparent.

There is a story about a Hasidic disciple and his lay partner, who was a very rational man. The disciple wanted very much for his partner to meet his Rebbe, but the young skeptic stubbornly refused. One day, however, the disciple managed to persuade his partner to attend a Sabbath dinner with the Rebbe.

During the meal, the disciple was surprised to see his friend's face light up in glee. When he later asked why he had been so moved, the partner replied: "When the Rebbe was eating, he looked like the High Priest at the time of the Temple, seated before the most holy sacrifice."

Not long after, the intrigued disciple sought out the rabbi to ask how a skeptic, on his first visit, could manage to see something the master's friends and followers hadn't seen. The rabbi explained, "He needed to see; the disciple needs to believe."

If you want to access the world of hiddenness and take advantage of it, you cannot arrive at certainty and legitimization through your sight. *Belief* is an external manifestation of the hidden realm. In fact, it is the only apparent representation that hiddenness can take on, because reason's pathways to the hidden realm are permanently blocked. Belief is the form that a hidden answer from the hidden realm takes on in the face of that which is apparent. Whether we are dealing with an intuition derived from the Apparent Realm of What Is Hidden or with an action prompted by the Hidden Realm of What Is Hidden, a discontinuity that allows the reasons for something to emerge only after direct experience has already convinced us.

Harvesting the fruit of this world is as essential as it is difficult—perhaps as difficult as parting the waters, as the rabbis would say. We find ourselves haunted by a sense of confusion when certainty precedes reason rather than following it, as its product. The sources of this certainty are the gamut of all possible systems of logic and the void surrounding any and all definitions, all identifications, and all particularizations of which our minds may be capable. Its wisdom lies in nonlimitation much more than in any specific, singular attribute. Yet it is not the void itself, for it is distinguishable by our mental faculties. Consider this story:

> The Rabbi of Volborz beheld an apparition of a recently deceased man whom he had known. The man was beseeching the rabbi to help him find a new wife, because his had died.
>
> "So you don't realize that you are no longer in the world of the living," the rabbi said—"that you are in a world of confusion?"
>
> When the man refused to believe this, the rabbi lifted the man's coat, revealing his shroud.
>
> When the rabbi's son heard what happened, he asked, "Well, in that case, who knows, maybe *I'm* in a world of confusion as well."

"Don't worry," his father replied. "As long as you are aware that such a world exists, you are not in it."

When you travel the hidden territory of what is hidden, you know that your knowledge does not come from the "world of confusion" precisely because you are aware of its existence. As long as you know this, as long as you do not relinquish your power of discernment due to your commitments, you cannot become part of the world of confusion. Belief and intuition—fruit of the Apparent Realm of What Is Hidden and of the Hidden Realm of What Is Hidden—are indissoluble parts of the orchard where reason and evidence also abide.

Whoever thinks intuits, and whoever thinks also believes: intuition and belief are inseparable parts of the process of organizing the world lying before us. They order the world through mediums, while discernment does so through defined forms.

As *Pirkei Avot* would put it, those who think with the purpose of doing—that is, with the purpose of venturing into the orchard of feelings to harvest what can nourish the world of existence—detect evidence and study it; but more to the point, further on they abandon this evidence, and based on what they have learned from it, they then intuit and believe in something that completes their knowledge. Their knowledge is composed of these two halves of an orange that actually do not fit together yet are part of the same unit: the mind.

EPILOGUE

The ultimate recipe for a complete journey through the orchard has been given to us in the daily liturgy of Jewish tradition. Among our many thanks for the blessings granted by our Creator, we express gratitude for the possibility of thinking. In this particular liturgy, known as *Ahavat Olam* (His Love of the World), God has offered us a closed orchard, an orchard full of meaning in and of itself. The text constitutes an outline of what we have analyzed in these pages. It tells us that the greatest of all gifts is the possibility of *lehavin u-le'askil; lish'moa, lilmod u-lelamed; lish'mor ve-la'assot; u-lekaiem*—"understanding and elucidating; listening, learning and teaching; safeguarding and performing; fulfilling." According to the text, this chain can illuminate our vision; we are granted a chance to see what is not visible thanks to the amazing resource of the orchard.

> *Understanding and elucidating:* These abilities afford us the ability to make crystal-clear judgments concerning things that appear in concrete and manifest form before us.

> *Listening, learning, and teaching:* These abilities allow us to use judgments in such a way that we can avoid personal and aesthetic mental blocks and grasp the bigger picture, reframed to reveal the hidden nature of things.

94

Safeguarding and performing: These are part of a world where experience overrides discernment. Safeguarding and performing do not enable a person to make permanent changes in behavior but do allow the individual at times to take actions without first filtering them through discernment and reason.

Fulfilling: This allows us to take everything we have explored theoretically and experienced practically and transform it into behavior, into part of what we are. What we think and what we discern are no longer abstract but become our very way of being.

The accompanying table shows how any problem can be broken down into four levels. In the area of discernment, of what is apparent in essence, we can reach what is hidden through ques-

DISCERNMENT (Left Hemisphere)	Apparent Realm of What Is Apparent	Understanding Elucidating	INFORMATION
	Hidden Realm of What Is Apparent	Listening Learning Teaching	UNDERSTANDING
COMMITMENT (Right Hemisphere)	Apparent Realm of What Is Hidden	Safeguarding Performing	WISDOM
	Hidden Realm of What Is Hidden	Fulfilling	REVERENCE

tions or ignorance. The greater you understand the extent of your ignorance, the more efficiently you can make decisions within this sphere of reason. On this plane, what is hidden is revealed not by producing answers but by reframing the question(s).

Within the area of commitment, of what is hidden, of what is ascertained empirically rather than by relying on reason, we can reach what is hidden by recognizing that experience not only yields data on life but also provides us with knowledge on the extent of our ignorances. The Hidden Realm of What Is Hidden is the principle of *acting first*, which makes us rethink the questions.

If you are armed with information, you can solve only those problems that are similar to others you have solved before. If you are armed with understanding, you can solve problems that require you to go back and explore the proposition, that is, the original question. If you are armed with wisdom, you can rely on your intuition and take action based on past experience, responding to new problems even before they appear. If you are armed with reverence, you can use your living experience to redirect your questions. In the first case, you know what you know; in the second, you know what you know and how much you don't know; in the third, you manage to "know" what you don't know; and in the last, you manage to "know" what you don't know and how much is left to be known.

It is not too hard to see what is meant by "information" and "understanding." We can also easily perceive what is meant by "wisdom"—although the notion is more complicated—and we can recognize its efficiency. But the notion of "reverence" is a highly complex one. If you act in reverence, it means you possess parameters regarding the main priorities and principles governing life. More and more problem-solvers are coming to understand that these four levels of skills are necessary. Corporations, for example, now believe that those who hold only information (and are easily replaced by machines) or only understanding (and are easily replaced by computers) don't make such good employees as those who know how to discern through living experience, those who take the chance of acting first rather than relying solely on reason. In displaying wisdom and acting in reverence, these individuals develop refined systems of ethics and are able to propose strategies and solutions for less immediate, longer-range questions. They ultimately manage to produce knowledge where there is none, supported by the extent of their ignorances.

Here is another classic Hasidic tale:

A man gets lost in the forest as darkness approaches. The darker it gets, the more upset he becomes. He eventually spies a lantern in the distance and breathes a sigh of relief that he has found someone. He heads toward the light, and when he reaches the man holding it aloft, he says, "It's so great to find you! I'm lost and it's already getting dark, but now everything's OK because you can show me the way out."

To this, the man with the lantern replies, "I'm sorry—I'm lost too. But don't be upset, because we know that where you came from and where I came from, there's no way out. So together we have more information and better chances of finding our way out."

The first man, who is not altogether convinced, studies the second man more closely and suddenly realizes he is blind. "But you can't see!" he exclaims. "Why do you need a lantern?"

"So *you* can see *me!*"

The apparent realm is represented by the man who is trying to find his way out of the forest; the hidden realm, by the blind man—who cannot see or "discern." Together they improve their chances. Light is the means by which *acting first* attracts *discerning first*. The only purpose the light serves for the blind man is to draw the attention of the other.

When our right hemisphere attempts to solve a problem, it doesn't use light to see, because it doesn't need it. Instead, it uses it to draw reason's attention, for reason always seeks light, that is, cognition. For the right hemisphere—for commitment—light is not an end in itself. As written in Psalm 36:10, "In Your light we shall see light." In other words, the purpose of the light is not to illuminate (understand, define, and solve) but to bring new light (new questions, new quests).

Perhaps the best way of exemplifying these four planes is found in the famous Jewish anecdote about a young man who wishes to study Talmud:

A young man in his mid-twenties knocks on the door of the noted scholar Rabbi Schwartz.

"My name is Sean Goldstein," he says. "I've come to you because I wish to study Talmud."

"Do you know Aramaic?" the rabbi asks.

"No."

"Hebrew?"

"No."

"Have you studied Torah?"

"No, Rabbi. But don't worry. I graduated Berkeley summa cum laude in philosophy, and just finished my doctoral dissertation at Harvard on Socratic logic. So now, I would just like to round out my education with a little study of the Talmud."

"I seriously doubt," the rabbi says, "that you are ready to study Talmud. It is the deepest book of our people. If you wish, however, I am willing to examine you in logic, and if you pass the test, I will teach you Talmud."

The young man agrees.

Rabbi Schwartz holds up two fingers. "Two men come down a chimney. One comes out with a clean face, the other comes out with a dirty face. Which one washes his face?"

The young man stares at the rabbi. "Is that the test in logic?"

The rabbi nods.

"The one with the dirty face washes his face," he answers wearily.

"Wrong. The one with the clean face washes his face. Examine the simple logic. The one with the dirty face looks at the one with the clean face and thinks his face is clean. The one with the clean face looks at the one with the dirty face and thinks his face is dirty. So the one with the clean face washes his face."

"Very clever," Goldstein says. "Give me another test."

The rabbi again holds up two fingers. "Two men come down a chimney. One comes out with a clean face, the other comes out with a dirty face. Which one washes his face?"

"We've already established that. The one with the clean face washes his face."

"Wrong. Each one washes his face. Examine the simple logic. The one with the dirty face looks at the one with the clean face and thinks his face is clean. The one with the clean face looks at the one with the dirty face and thinks his face is dirty. So the one with the clean face washes his face. When the one with the dirty face sees the one with the clean face wash his face, he also washes his face. So each one washes his face."

"I didn't think of that," says Goldstein. "It's shocking to me that I could make an error in logic. Test me again."

The rabbi holds up two fingers. "Two men come down a chimney. One comes out with a clean face, the other comes out with a dirty face. Which one washes his face?"

"Each one washes his face."

"Wrong. Neither one washes his face. Examine the simple logic. The one with the dirty face looks at the one with the clean face and thinks his face is clean. The one with the clean face looks at the one with the dirty face and thinks his face is dirty. But when the one with the clean face sees that the one with the dirty face doesn't wash his face, he also doesn't wash his face. So neither one washes his face."

Goldstein is desperate. "I am qualified to study Talmud. Please give me one more test."

He groans, though, when the rabbi lifts two fingers. "Two men come down a chimney. One comes out with a clean face, the other comes out with a dirty face. Which one washes his face?"

"Neither one washes his face."

"Wrong. Do you now see, Sean, why Socratic logic is an insufficient basis for studying Talmud? Tell me, how is it possible for two men to come down the same chimney, and for one to come out with a clean face and the other with a dirty face? Don't you see? The whole question is *narishkeit*—foolishness—and if you spend your life trying to answer foolish questions, all your answers will also be foolish."[14]

The Apparent Realm of What Is Apparent is represented by the answer "The one with the dirty face washes his face." The Hidden Realm of What Is Apparent is represented by the interpretation that one looks at the other and the one with the clean face washes his. Seeing this hidden realm means recognizing the human trait of always looking at the Other and understanding oneself through him or her. The Apparent Realm of What Is Hidden is represented in the other two possibilities: "Both wash their faces" and "Neither does." In both of these cases, in addition to discerning reality through what is seen in the Other, the men do as the other even though their actions might not make sense. Understanding the question from this angle means using wisdom and a deep knowledge of human nature much more than a theoretical discernment of logic. Lastly, the Hidden Realm of What Is Hidden can be found in the final interpretation—"How silly!"—where we are brought back to the original question by a

---

14. Rabbi Joseph Telushkin, *Jewish Humor: What the Best Jewish Jokes Say about the Jews* (New York: William Morrow and Co., 1992, 1998), pp. 47–48. © 1992 by Joseph Telushkin. Used by permission of William Morrow & Co., Inc.

desire to take another look at the proposition itself based on our experience: "If you go into a chimney, your face will get dirty." Reverence is displayed when contact with reality, with life, takes precedence. It is essential to not let ourselves get carried away by conceptual aspects and always to check the appropriateness of our discernment by filtering it through our experience. Many problems can be solved by recognizing their irrelevance— leaving us free to devote ourselves to more important issues. We learn to properly revere that which is relevant.

What is indispensable is for us to recognize that this world is not self-evident. The visible is nothing more than a path to revealing the invisible—light serving to disclose the hidden light of light itself.